Interfaith Dialogues and Debates

Also by Ahmed Lotfy Rashed

What Would a Muslim Say?
Top 15 Tough Questions on Islam
The Qur'an Discussions

Interfaith Dialogues and Debates
What Would a Muslim Say?
Volume 3

by

Ahmed Lotfy Rashed

Common Word Publishing
"With Dialogue Comes Understanding"

Copyright

Copyright © 2018 by Ahmed Lotfy Rashed

All rights reserved. This book or any portion thereof may not be reproduced or used in any manner whatsoever without the express written permission of the publisher, except for the use of brief quotations in a book review.

Editing: Allister Thompson

Cover Design: Stewart Williams

ISBN–13: 978-0999431818

Dedication

In the Name of God,
the Most-Gracious,
the Ever-Merciful.

Acknowledgments

There are many people to thank for this book:

First, I thank my mother for teaching me always to be patient, even if it is uncomfortable. And I thank my father for teaching me always to be truthful, even if it is unpopular.

Second, I thank my wife for her patience, support, and encouragement as I navigated each conversation.

Last, but certainly not least, I want to thank the shining models whom I consulted or referenced for the more nuanced or detailed answers that I had to provide: Yasir Qadhi, Gai Eaton, Zaid Shakir, Hamza Yusuf, Nouman Ali Khan, Suhaib Webb, Sherman Jackson, and Jamal Badawi. May God bless you all and preserve your teachings for all students of Islam.

Contents

Copyright iv
Dedication v
Acknowledgments vi
Contents vii
Introduction 3
    The Conversations Continue 4
Conversation With Kerry 7
    The Islamic Worldview and Ethics 7
Conversation With Nancy 17
    The Apostasy Debate 17
Conversation With Roland 29
    What Is Creation For? 29
Conversation With Denise 33
    A Better Understanding in Forty-Two Questions 33
Conversation With Roger 53
    The Islam and Peace Debate 53
Conversation With Neil 71
    The Remembrance of God 71
Conversation With Mark 77
    The Shroud of Turin Debate 77
Conversation With Trevon 89
    Why Is There Confilct in the Middle East? 89
Conversation With Chris 99
    A Muslim–Christian Dialogue 99
A Message from the Author 136
Islamic Law, Theology, and Practice 138

About the Author xii

TOUGH QUESTIONS AND HONEST ANSWERS ABOUT THE WORLD'S FASTEST-GROWING AND MOST CONTROVERSIAL FAITH

TOP 15 TOUGH QUESTIONS ON ISLAM

AHMED LOTFY RASHED

Get your FREE copy when you sign up to the author's email list!

**GET IT HERE:
WhatWouldAMuslimSay.net**

MY TEACHER WAS AHMED RASHED. WE SPENT A LOT OF TIME GOING THROUGH THE QUR'AN. AFTER THAT I STARTED TO UNDERSTAND MUSLIMS MUCH BETTER.
—FORMER ISLAM-101 STUDENT

Interfaith Dialogues and Debates

Introduction

Introduction

The Conversations Continue

This book contains conversations with people who reached out to WhyIslam.org for dialogue and received me as their correspondent. WhyIslam conversations typically begin when a person visits the WhyIslam website and submits a "One to One Email Correspondence" form. From this form, the Correspondence Manager assigns the visitor to one of the WhyIslam volunteers. Once assigned, the questions or comments are delivered to my email, and I then initiate the first email to reach out and respond to the visitor's questions. The conversation flows from there, just like a print letter correspondence.

This volume is a continuation of my first book, *What Would a Muslim Say?* and contains conversations from 2011 to 2016. In this volume, the correspondents are devout Christians. Some are ecumenical and sympathetic, some are evangelical and confrontational, and some are in between. The conversations in this book are real. They are faithful transcripts of email correspondence I have had with WhyIslam.org visitors over the years. To protect the privacy of our visitors, the names and identifying details have been changed. That email is reproduced here for reference.

Standard Email Introduction

Email #01 – From: Ahmed Rashed

In the Name of God, the Most-Gracious, the Ever-Merciful:
Thank you for taking the time to contact us and learn about Islam straight from the source. We practice and promote a balanced view of Islam — the "middle way" that the Qur'an calls Muslims to follow: a path of moderation that is free of *extremism*.

Before we begin, let me introduce myself. My name is Ahmed Rashed. I was born in Egypt but raised in America. I am married with three little children. I work as a test software engineer, but my life passion is teaching others about Islam.

Now I'm going to give you a brief description of what Islam is all about: Islam is not a new religion. Rather, it is the same truth that God revealed through all His prophets to every people. For over a fifth of the world's population, Islam is both a religion and a complete way of life. Muslims are taught to be truthful, to be just, to help the needy, to honor their parents, and to maintain good relations with neighbors and relatives.

The Qur'an tells Muslims to say: "We believe in God and what was revealed to us, and what was revealed to Abraham and Ishmael and Isaac and Jacob and the Tribes, and what was given to Moses and Jesus and to the Prophets from their Lord. We do not separate between them, and to Him we submit." (3:84)

This is how Islam sees itself in relation to all other religions. The Message revealed to Muhammad is considered God's religion for humanity in its final form. Muslims view Muhammad as the final successor to Jesus, Moses, Abraham, and all the previous prophets. Muslims view the Qur'an as the final Testament from God to humanity. Just as God sent revelation to Moses and Jesus (peace be upon them), Muslims believe God sent revelation to Muhammad (peace be upon him) to confirm, correct, and complete all previous Scriptures.

The Qur'an says that God sent prophets to every community in history. These prophets were men of high moral character chosen by God to teach their people about their duty to God and to their fellow man. The Qur'an teaches that this duty was always "submission and devotion to God" and to treat all God's creation with equality and compassion.

"Islam" is simply the Arabic word for this duty of "submission and devotion" to God.

"Muslim" is the Arabic word for "one who submits" to God and obeys Him.

The Qur'an says that whenever a people broke away from God's teachings, God would send another prophet to bring them back to His Path. This is how Muslims understand the many prophets sent to the Children of Israel and the many religions in the world today.

Introduction

Prophet Muhammad, like all the prophets before him, called people to believe in and worship One God, to believe in His angels, to believe in His prophets, to believe in His revelations, to believe in the Day of Judgment, and to believe in Divine Decree and Destiny.

Prophet Muhammad, like all the prophets before him, called people to bear witness that there is no god but God and that he was God's Messenger, to pray regularly, to give charity regularly, and to fast as a form of self-purification. Prophet Muhammad, like Prophet Abraham before him, called people to make the pilgrimage to the Holy Sanctuary in Mecca, where the first house of worship dedicated to God Almighty was built.

This is just a general overview, so please reply with any questions you may have. I look forward to your response, and I hope to continue the discussion.

May peace be with you,
Ahmed Rashed

Conversation with Kerry

The Islamic Worldview and Ethics

Email #02 – From: Kerry
Sent: Monday, September 12, 2011 11:28 a.m.

Is there some problem Muslims have with Jews? I kind of understand the Palestine/Israel conflict, but it seems like the tension between the two goes deeper.

Email #03 – From: Ahmed Rashed
Sent: Monday, September 12, 2011 4:18 p.m.

In the Name of God, the Most-Gracious, the Ever-Merciful:
Jews were able to live in peace and prosperity and intellectual freedom under the rule of the Muslims in the Middle Ages. In fact, the Golden Age of Jewish Philosophy was simultaneous with the Golden Age of Muslim Rule. When the Inquisition swept through Spain and when the Crusaders swept through Jerusalem, it was to neighboring Muslim lands that Jews fled and found haven and a new life. In Europe, while Muslims were never able to live as Muslims, and Jews were only marginally able to live as Jews, it is a historical fact that Jews, Christians, Buddhists, and Hindus were able to live their faiths in Muslim lands.

It is an integral part of Islamic law that all people have the right to live and practice their faith, even if that faith is not Islam. The Prophet specifically said that anyone who violates the rights of a Jew or Christian living in Muslim lands will never smell the fragrance of Paradise. The current conflict is all about land rights and heritage, not religious difference.

If I may ask, what led to your impression that "the tension between the two goes deeper?"

May peace be with you,
Ahmed

Email #04 – From: Kerry
Sent: Tuesday, September 13, 2011 2:21 p.m.

I guess it's because it seems every Muslim I talk to has a bit of a problem with both Jews and Christians. I figured it was just a matter of the opinion of that person.

On another topic, do you know where I could find the ninety-nine names of Allah?

Email #05 – From: Ahmed Rashed
Sent: Thursday, September 15, 2011 11:00 a.m.

In the Name of God, the Most-Gracious, the Ever-Merciful:

Well, theologically, there is the idea that what Jews and Christians now follow is not what Moses and Jesus originally preached. The Qur'an clearly states that all prophets preached the same message of God's Unity and His right to be worshiped. It also clearly states that all prophets preached that men should act with compassion and justice on Earth. However, the Qur'an also states that most of the details of these authentic divine teachings were distorted or changed after those prophets left this world.

For this reason, just as Christians reach out to Jews with the "New Testament" from God so as to keep their Covenant with Him valid, Muslims reach out to Jews and Christians with the "Final Testament" from God so as to keep their Covenant with Him valid.

Muslims see themselves as the recipients of the Final Revelation from God and that this revelation has not been corrupted by human hands. For this reason, the Qur'an refers to Jews and Christians as "People of the Book" instead of just "disbelievers." The Qur'an acknowledges that they did receive authentic messengers from God and that they did at one point have authentic Scripture that was God's Word; however, that Original Word was hidden, lost, forgotten, added to, or changed by the hands of men.

So even though we invite all people to accept Islam, we do not coerce or force or cajole. We let our neighbors know about the divine guidance that we have received and then it is up to them to accept or reject. That is between them and God. Regardless of whether a person accepts Islam or not, he is still from the progeny of Adam and a full human being with all the dignity and rights that this implies. On the personal level, Muslims are required to treat all human beings with respect and dignity. Only in the face of aggression against faith or home does a Muslim have the right to fight and use lethal force to defend himself.

As for the Ninety-Nine Names of Allah, here are a few websites that give a good description:

http://www.islamicity.com/mosque/99names.htm
http://www.jannah.org/articles/names.html

Feel free to reply with any questions or comments you may have.

May peace be with you,
Ahmed

Email #06 – From: Kerry
Sent: Friday, September 16, 2011 11:01 a.m.

What are the principal rules that regulate a moderate Muslim's life?

Email #07 – From: Ahmed Rashed
Sent: Tuesday, September 20, 2011 9:17 a.m.

The Islamic lifestyle can be summarized by the following passage in the Qur'an: **Say, "Come, let me tell you what your Lord has forbidden you: that you associate nothing with Him; that you honor your parents; that you do not kill your children because of poverty—We provide for you and for them; that you do not come near adultery, whether outward or inward; and that you do not kill the soul which God has sanctified—except in the course of justice. All this He has enjoined upon you, so that you may understand."**

And do not come near the property of the orphan, except with the best intentions, until he reaches maturity. And give full weight and full measure, equitably. We do not burden any soul beyond its capacity. And when you speak, be just, even if it concerns a close relative. And fulfill your covenant with God. All this He has enjoined upon you, so that you may take heed. (6:151-152)

So this passage highlights the major "commandments" in Islam. Here is the breakdown and explanation of each point:

Do not take any other god before God. This is the same First Commandment as in the Bible.

Honor your parents. This is also nearly identical to the Bible. Parental obedience and dutifulness is integral to Islam. The preservation of family ties is a fundamental principle of Islam, along with kind treatment of orphans, widows, travelers, and neighbors. The Qur'an says: **"And your Lord has decreed that you worship none but Him. And that you be kind to your parents. If one of them or both of them attain old age in your life, say not to them a word of contempt, nor repel them, but address them in terms of honor."** (17:23)

However, Muslims are not obligated to obey their parents if they command idolatry or other sins: **"But if they strive to make you join in worship with Me others of which you have no knowledge, then obey them not, but behave kindly with them in the world."** (31:15)

Do not kill your children out of fear of poverty. This was a common practice in seventh century Arabia, and the Prophet strongly condemned it. This is also why most Muslims oppose abortion.

Do not approach adultery, either openly or privately. This is where sexual morality comes in. This is very similar to Judaism and Christianity but with more explicit rules. When it comes to dressing and behavior, modesty and humility are ordained for both men and women. Muhammad (pbuh) has stated, *"Every religion has an essential character and the essential character of Islam is modesty."* God says in the Qur'an **"And do not approach adultery; truly it is shameful indecency and an evil path." (17:34)**

From this, we understand that not only is sex outside of marriage a sin, but even coming near to this act is also a sin. For this reason, the Prophet instructed his community to be very modest around the opposite sex. That is why Muslim men and women cover so much of their bodies in public.

Do not commit murder. The general rule in Islam is that all life is sacred; only in pursuit of justice is it permissible to shed blood. Muslim scholars define the "cause of justice" as follows:
1. It is permissible to implement capital punishment for capital crimes such as treason, murder, armed robbery, etc.
2. It is permissible to use lethal force in self-defense or defense of one's home or family.
3. It is permissible for soldiers to kill other soldiers on the battlefield.

As mentioned earlier, the terrorist acts committed by Muslims are nothing more than simple cold-blooded murder. They are **not** legitimate warfare and certainly **not** self-defense.

Do not exploit orphans or their wealth. This was another common problem at the time of the Prophet, so many verses were revealed admonishing the Arabs for their exploitation of the weak and disadvantaged in society.

Give full weight and measure. This means the ethics of buying and selling. Islam teaches that all economic interactions should be honest and free of deceit or fraud. This means that all sellers must make clear to the buyer exactly what is being purchased and must fully disclose any faults of their merchandise. Also, a person should not earn his money at the expense of another, so Islam forbids stealing, gambling, and interest.

Stealing is forbidden because the thief gains a good without fair compensation to the rightful owner. Gambling is forbidden because it is a system whereby many lose so that one or few win. It also fosters enmity and hatred among people, as mentioned in the prohibition of alcohol. Interest is forbidden because it is a system by which the rich get richer at the expense of the poor getting poorer. This is directly opposite to the Islamic institution of Zakat and the aims of charity.

Be just in speech. This describes how Muslims are supposed to interact with other people. In particular, the Qur'an highlights some of the manners and values a Muslim is supposed to display:

And do good to parents, relatives, orphans, the poor, the neighbor who is near of kin, the neighbor who is a stranger, the companion by your side, the wayfarer, and those whom your right hand possess. (4:36)

O you who believe! Be steadfast in the cause of God and bear witness with justice. Do not let your enmity for others turn you away from justice. Deal justly; that is nearer to being God-fearing. And fear God, for God is aware of all that you do. (5:8)

Do not avert your face from people out of haughtiness and do not walk with pride on the earth: for verily God does not love arrogant and boastful people. (31:18)

O you who believe! Let not some men among you ridicule others: it may be that the latter are better than the former: nor should some women laugh at others: it may be that the latter are better than the former.

And do not defame or be sarcastic to each other, or call each other by evil names. How bad it is to earn an evil reputation after accepting the faith! Those who do not repent are evil-doers.

O you who believe! Avoid much suspicion. Indeed some suspicion is a sin. And do not spy on one another and do not backbite. Would any of you like to eat his dead brother's flesh? No, you would hate it. Fear God, and God is ever forgiving and most merciful. (49:11-12)

In addition, the Prophetic sayings highlight some of the manners a Muslim is supposed to display:

"The most beloved to God are those with the best manners."

"Having a sense of modesty is one branch of faith."

"Whoever cheats or deceives is not one of us."

"A person who does not keep his promise has no religion."

"God will show no compassion to he who shows no compassion to others."

"None of you truly believes until he wishes for his brother what he wishes for himself."

"He who truly believes in God and the Last Day should say what is good or keep silent."

"Foul language and harsh behavior is injustice, and the home of injustice is Hell."

"The strong man is not he who can knock the other down; the strong man is he who can control himself when angry."

Finally, the Muslim's dietary restrictions are to avoid of pork, alcohol, intoxicants, and anything slaughtered in a name other than God.

Feel free to reply with any questions or comments or with any other topic you wish to discuss.

May peace be with you,
Ahmed

Email #08 – From: Kerry
Sent: Wednesday, September 21, 2011 11:57 a.m.

Where are the sayings of the Prophet Muhammad found?

Email #09 – From: Ahmed Rashed
Sent: Friday, September 23, 2011 8:22 a.m.

There are many books that record the Prophet's sayings. Most Muslims reference Bukhari and Muslim's books. They are still in circulation today and are considered the two most authentic and authoritative books of sayings by Muslim scholars and laity. You can also check out this link for a more expansive description of how the sayings were memorized, compiled, and **preserved.**
http://islamicsciences.wordpress.com/2006/12/14/the-preservation-of-hadith-over-the-generations/

As usual, feel free to reply with questions, clarification, or discussion.

May peace be with you,
Ahmed

With Dialogue Comes Understanding

Conversation with Nancy

The Apostasy Debate

Email #02 – From: Nancy
Sent: Thursday, September 29, 2011 7:38 a.m.

Islam is confusing. Right now Iran is going to execute a Christian pastor, all because he refused to recant his Christian beliefs and convert to Islam. Islam is forcing him to convert to Islam. Islam therefore is a vile religion.

http://www.foxnews.com/world/2011/09/28/iranian-pastor-faces-execution-for-refusing-to-recant-christian-faith/

This is why Islam cannot be the religion of peace, as you try to claim. I'm not talking about terrorists; I'm talking about duly elected governments. Even in Pakistan, Egypt, and all these Muslim countries — all they think about is killing people who don't follow their way of thinking. Islam is like the mafia, and I am sorry, but you are telling the West a pack of lies about Islam. I know Muslims who have converted to Christianity and are persecuted mercilessly by your clerics.

Email #03 – From: Ahmed Rashed
Sent: Thursday, September 29, 2011 11:09 a.m.

In the Name of God, the Most-Gracious, the Ever-Merciful:

We do not believe that Islam calls for death for apostasy. There is a death penalty for certain crimes, but it has nothing to do with simple apostasy and will be made clear later in this text. This is a long response, so please be patient and read to the end.

Islam, like any other religion, has many different interpretations. I will admit that some classical Islamic texts insist on death for apostasy. However, these texts were written by fallible human beings based on interpretations that are NOT SUPPORTED BY THE QUR'AN. Al-Azhar University, which was and continues to be one of the foremost authorities on Islam, issued a fatwa confirming this in 1958.

When the Ottoman Empire united the Islamic empire under single leadership, it officially abolished any death penalties for apostates that were in place at the time. At this point, it wasn't widely practiced at all, but the Ottomans made it officially illegal. The caliph — who was the ultimate authority at the time — pointed out that the Qur'an didn't support this punishment and that close inspection of related sayings of the Prophet (the *Hadith*) show there is no support there either. While there are Hadith that support the death penalty for apostasy, it is only in cases where apostasy is combined with treason against the state.

At the time, the Ottomans were attempting to reform old practices and bring Islam back to what it was intended to be, without cultural interference. The National Law of 1869, for example, guaranteed all citizens equality under the law regardless of ethnicity or religion. Their justification was that the Qur'an never states that apostates should be killed. That's the bottom line. On the contrary, the Qur'an states, **"Let there be no compulsion in religion: truth is distinct from error." (2:256)**

Every Muslim knows this verse, and many scholars use it to argue that there should not be any death penalty for those who leave Islam. God is telling us that people have free will and freedom of choice. Here is the context of that verse: a man named Husayn bin Salim bin Awf had two daughters. Both of them were Christians. He attempted to persuade them to Islam, but they declined. He then went to the Prophet (pbuh) and asked him for permission to force his daughters into Islam. This verse was revealed in response and forbade parents from forcing their children into a specific religion.

Further, the Qur'an states, **"And if your Lord had pleased, surely all those who are in the earth would have believed; will you then force men till they become believers?" (10:99)**

God is saying here that Muslims should worry about themselves and their own relationship with God, not other people's choices: **"And had God willed, He could have made you all one community, but He leaves astray whom He wills and guides whom He wills. But you shall certainly be called to account for what you used to do." (16:93)**

The concepts in this verse are repeated many times in the Qur'an; no one can force people into religion. Why then would GOD instruct the believers to kill someone for leaving a religion? How does that possibly make sense? And yet another verse: **"Exhort them to believe; your task is only to exhort. You cannot compel them to believe." (88:21-22)**

There are people during the time of the Prophet (pbuh) that believed then disbelieved. The Qur'an does not say to kill them when it discusses these people. Rather, it says, **"Those who believe then disbelieve, again believe and again disbelieve, then increase in disbelief, Allah will never forgive them nor guide them to the Way." (4:137)**

The punishment is in the afterlife, period. It's God's punishment, not Man's punishment. Now let us turn to the Hadith. A lot of times, people quote part of a Hadith that says, *"Whoever changes his religion, kill him."* When you just look at this excerpt, it seems that the Prophet taught the death penalty for apostasy. The problem is that this Hadith is *incomplete*. Just as biblical texts need context, Islamic texts do too. The phrase I quoted above never came from the Prophet (pbuh) himself; rather, it came from a man named Ibn Abbas.

In this Hadith, he is **paraphrasing** the Prophet (pbuh), not directly quoting him. (See Sahih Bukhari, Vol. 9, Book 84, Number 57) More importantly, this Hadith is not referring to peaceful apostasy but rather those who rejected Islam and joined the enemy forces, using treachery to rebel against the Muslim army and kill as many people as possible.

So what were the exact words of the Prophet? Do we have any other authentic sayings of the Prophet that are actual direct quotes? Yes, we do. He said, "The blood of a Muslim, who confesses that there is no god but God and that I am His Apostle, cannot be shed except in three cases: (1) In penalty for murder, (2) a married person who commits adultery and (3) the one who apostates from Islam and leaves the community." (Sahih Bukhari, Vol. 12, Book ad-Diyat, Number 6878, p. 209)

So there are three instances in which capital punishment is justified: (1) murdering another, (2) committing adultery, and (3) apostasy *combined* with **leaving the community**. Leaving the community can be further explained when we look even closer at the issue in another Hadith: "The blood of a Muslim, who confesses that none has the right to be worshiped but God and that I am His Apostle, cannot be shed except in three cases: (1) a married person who commits adultery; he is to be stoned and (2) a man who went out fighting against God and His Messenger; he is to be killed or crucified or exiled from the land; and (3) a man who murders another person; he is to be killed in punishment of it." (Sunan Abu Dawud, Vol. 4, Number 4353, p. 126)

The same three instances appear in both Hadith, but the Abu Dawud narration is more explicit than the Bukhari narration. Leaving the community refers to a man who changed sides and fought against the Muslims — basically committing treason, **NOT** someone who changed his mind and no longer believes in Islam. Anyone who advocates executing an ex-Muslim simply on the basis of their change in beliefs is clearly **violating** the teachings of the Prophet (pbuh).

At the time of the Prophet (pbuh) there was open, declared war between the pagans of Mecca and the Muslims of Medina. Some Muslims apostatized at this time because they feared the numerical superiority of the Meccan army. However, the real problem was a group who joined the Muslims with the intention of abandoning them when the Meccans invaded Medina. The opinion of a several classical and contemporary scholars is that the killing of apostates was only in reference to *these* people who converted for the purpose of betraying the Muslims. Peaceful apostasy was not punished as long as the people didn't pick up arms against the Muslims. They continued to live in the community, whether they were Christians or Jews or pagan. Ultimately, nobody can make a case for killing apostates without ignoring the verses of the Qur'an that call for tolerance and forbid compulsion.

Conversation With Nancy

One of God's gifts to humanity is the gift of speech. It is through dialogue that we can come to greater understanding and peaceful relations. I look forward to your reply so we may continue the discussion and address any other concerns you may have.

May peace be with you,
Ahmed

Email #04 – From: Nancy
Sent: Wednesday, February 22, 2012 3:29 p.m.

I have read your long reply, but your arguments leave so much room for interpretation. *"While there are Hadith that support the death penalty for apostasy, it is only in cases where apostasy is combined with treason against the state."* What is this??

What constitutes "treason against the state" is open to wide interpretation. Talking to a Muslim about Christ could be interpreted as treason against the state. If a Muslim converts to Christianity and knows that more Muslims are dying without knowing the saving grace of God through Jesus Christ, he of course should be allowed to talk about his new faith with other Muslims. That is the essence of "freedom of religion." Muslims should have the freedom to read the Bible, to be free to accept or reject Jesus Christ. The state should have no business in deciding for me what religion I should follow. It is none of their business because it is a personal decision between me and my God.

Right now, a Christian pastor is going to die because he refused to revert back to Islam. This is just like the Spanish Inquisition, but in this case, your Holy Books, the Hadith, prescribe this treatment. That is what is so shameful and diabolical about Islam. Islam has no compassion, no mercy as far as anyone with a brain can see.

http://www.foxnews.com/world/2012/02/22/iran-court-convicts-christian-pastor-convert-to-death/

Read this article and tell me if Islam has a heart or not. This is why I cannot see Islam as a peaceful religion but rather a religion of death. Christianity, it seems to me, is the superior religion because Christ never killed anyone. He never beheaded anyone, but Muhammad has blood on his hands. When he stands before the judgment throne of God, he will be called to answer for it. These Iranians and you as a Muslim will also one day stand before the Almighty with blood on your hands because you didn't do anything to stop the deliberate execution of an innocent man whose only crime is to leave Islam. Shame on Islam.

Nancy

Email #05 – From: Ahmed Rashed
Sent: Thursday, February 23, 2012 9:52 a.m.

In the Name of God, the Most-Gracious, the Ever-Merciful:

Thank you for replying. However, we must disagree with you. There is no room for interpretation. I quoted the exact words of the Prophet. The point of our response is that the death sentence in this news article is NOT LAWFUL according the mainstream understanding of Muslim scholars around the world.

In fact, in the Qur'an, Prophet Muhammad is given these instructions: **Say, "O people, the truth has come to you from your Lord. Whoever accepts guidance is guided for his own soul; and whoever strays only strays to its detriment. I am not a guardian over you." (10:108)**

So if the Prophet himself is not appointed as a keeper to enforce faith over people, then who in the world do these governments think they are to appoint themselves as keepers over people?

A man by the name Qurra b. Maysara, for instance, apostatized from Islam, but the Messenger (pbuh) sent nobody after him. 'Abd Allah b. Sa'd b. Abi al-Sarh also apostatized during his time, but he was also not attacked. Also, a man by the name Dhu al-Khuwaysira al-Tamimi, after accusing the Prophet (pbuh) of unjustly dividing the spoils of war, was let go to live the remainder of his life free of harm as a pagan. If there was some religious obligation to kill apostates under all circumstances, we would have seen the Messenger himself seek them out. The truth, however, is that because such people posed no danger to the security of the new Islamic polity, the Prophet (pbuh) allowed them to follow their conscience that led them to adopt other metaphysical understandings.

So while we admit that there are Muslim governments and Muslim people who condemn ex-Muslims to death and using the teachings of the Prophet for justification, we believe that they are WRONG, like those who commit acts of terrorism and use the teachings of Islam to justify those acts. This is not only the opinion of mainstream American Muslim scholars; it is also the opinion of Sheikh Ali Gomaa, grand mufti of Egypt. You can see the statements of other respected scholars on this issue here:

http://apostasyandislam.blogspot.com/

Remember: with dialogue comes understanding.

May peace be with you,

Ahmed

Email #06 – From: Nancy
Sent: Friday, February 24, 2012 5:31 p.m.

Thank you for your prompt reply. I understand what you are saying, but until American Muslims come out in force and condemn Muslim governments for executing people for apostasy, and who have not taken arms against Muslims, it's very difficult for anyone to accept the truth of Islam. Proselytizing Christianity to other Muslims is not taking arms against Muslims. But that is exactly why Iran has condemned this pastor to death. Just like Muslims in this country are free to proselytize Islam, likewise, Muslim converts to Christ should freely proselytize to other Muslims anywhere in the world. How else will they come to know Jesus Christ?

My difficulty is the actions of Muslims speak far louder than words you use to convince me. I have yet to hear CAIR or any Muslim organization gather in front of Muslim embassies condemning the violence against the Coptic Christians and their churches. Where is Sheikh Ali Gomaa, grand mufti of Egypt, when it came to the slaughter of Coptic Christians? Nothing was reported in the major networks of the Sheikh coming to the defense of the Coptic Christians in Egypt. So again, it's only words. Even here in the US, when a Muslim converts to Christianity, his/her life is in danger by people in the mosque, by their family and friends. I can understand them being upset about it, but to threaten his/her life? Really, why don't they teach tolerance for apostates in the mosques like you tell me Muhammad did? After all, Muslims around the world demand tolerance for Islam.

I'm also surprised to learn that Christ is mentioned many times in the Koran and yet Muslims do not know him personally. Shouldn't Muslims read the Bible to get a better picture of who Christ really is? Perhaps if Muslims know Christ personally, they will come to understand that He is God who came down to Earth in a time-space dimension and completed his ministry in just three years of preaching. And then he was crucified, died, and was buried. On the third day, he rose again and his teachings spread despite centuries of people who tried to kill it. Now that, to me, is a God thing. Jesus didn't take a sword or was the head of an army or beheaded anyone who didn't subject themselves to his cause. Unlike Muhammad, through kindness, love, compassion, and mercy, his words and his presence still attract people because Jesus was and is God. He was perfect and knew no sin. If that isn't God, I don't know what is.

Thank you for taking time to read my letters. I appreciate our dialogue.

Blessings,
Nancy

Email #07 – From: Ahmed Rashed
Sent: Monday, February 27, 2012 10:45 a.m.

Dear Nancy,

Did you read all of my previous email? I provided a link that shows **over one hundred scholars around the world** (including the former grand mufti of Al-Azhar University in Egypt) **condemning such sentences**. *Every major mainstream Islamic scholar* around the world has been condemning these government-sanctioned and extrajudicial executions. As for your concern about Copts in Egypt, I can assure you as an Egyptian who regularly watches the Egyptian channel news, there have been sheikhs publicly condemning those attacks.

The REAL PROBLEM is that the sheer volume of media propaganda and misinformation against Islam drowns out the mainstream Muslim voice. While it is true that some Muslims and some Muslim governments do evil deeds, it is also true that certain media outlets emphasize those evil acts without balancing what the religion *actually* **preaches**. Bad Muslims are bad Muslims. Bad governments are bad governments. We denounce them both.

As for CAIR not issuing a condemnation, that is not in their scope. They are a political group who deal with *American* Islamic relations. They are not international. Your accusations are not fair, because CAIR posts press release after press release about domestic civil rights issues, not foreign issues. Please read this article, because Mr. Eteraz expressed the point much better than I could:

http://www.huffingtonpost.com/ali-eteraz/the-myth-of-muslim-condem_b_67904.html

As for why Muslims do not learn more about Jesus Christ (peace and blessings be upon him), the answer is that Jesus is the second-most mentioned Prophet in the Qur'an after Moses (peace be upon them both). The story of Jesus is told in many places, and his works and message are emphasized throughout.

The Prophet Muhammad (pbuh) said, *"If anyone testifies that None has the right to be worshipped but God Alone, without partners, and that Muhammad is His Servant and His Messenger, and that Jesus is God's Servant and His Messenger and His Word which He bestowed on Mary and a Spirit created by Him, and that Paradise is true, and that Hell is true — God will admit him into Paradise with the deeds which he had done, even if those deeds were few."*

So Muslims also call Jesus (pbuh) the Word of God, but we understand that to refer to the fact that God said, *"Be!"* and Jesus was created in the womb of Mary (peace be upon her) without any man touching her.

As for why Muhammad had an army and fought battles and sentenced criminals, the real question should be why Jesus did not do these things. Moses (pbuh) commanded armies. He sentenced criminals to death or punishment. He fought battles. So did Joshua and David and Solomon and other Hebrew prophets. Why? Why did Jesus and some other prophets (like Abraham or Jacob or Joseph) not do this? The answer is not due to what each prophet wanted or desired but rather due to the circumstances that each prophet lived in and what God's Wisdom commanded each particular prophet to do.

Jesus lived in a time and place where there was established authority, so he was not commanded to rebel against that authority. Moses and Joshua and David and Solomon and Muhammad, in contrast, did not live in such a time or place. They were charged by God to ESTABLISH such an authority. They were political as well as spiritual leaders, responsible for material security as well as spiritual felicity.

Again, please accept my apologies for the lengthy email, and I look forward to your response.

May peace be with you,
Ahmed

With Dialogue Comes Understanding

Conversation With Roland

What Is Creation For?

Email #02 – From: Roland
Sent: Sunday, October 2, 2011 1:18 p.m.

Dear Ahmed,

What is creation for? Is it just an experiment on God's part? Is it an amusement or a playful diversion? If God is perfect, then why does he need us as, imperfect as we are? Of course, he could correct us, but is he waiting for us to self-correct individually? Is it beyond us, or did He tell us and we missed the point? Stand firm in faith, as it is all any of us can have. We can do good things here, and things can turn out good eventually.

Best Regards,
Roland

Email #03 – From: Ahmed Rashed
Sent: Tuesday, October 4, 2011 2:50 p.m.

In the Name of God, the Most-Gracious, the Ever-Merciful:

Dear Roland,

For today's materialist, life holds little significance other than that of consumption and seeking instant gratification. To believers in God and His Divine Unity, however, life is seen as a rich tapestry of signs and as an arena of tests that afford us the opportunity of knowing Allah and worshiping Him: **"I created men and jinn only that they may worship Me." (51:56)**

Early Qur'an exegetists have cited Ibn 'Abbås and his illustrious student, Mujåhid, as saying that Allah's words: **'that they may worship Me'** — *illå li ya'budun*, actually means: **'that they may know Me'** — *illå li ya'rifun*. The reason for this is quite straightforward: we cannot worship Allah without first knowing Him.

In his essay on divine love, **Ibn Rajab al-Hanbali** wrote: *"Allah created creation so that they may worship Him through love, fear and hope of Him. Allah, Exalted is He, said:* **'I created jinn and men only that they may worship Me.'** *However, Allah can only be worshiped by possessing knowledge (ma'rifah) of Him; which is why He* created the heavens and the earth, and all that is between them, as an indicator to His divinity and majesty. About this, Allah proclaims: *'Allah it is who has created seven heavens, and of the earth a similar number. His command descends through them, so that you may know Allah has power over all things, and that He encompasses all things in knowledge.'(65:12)* Here we are told that creation was created 'that you may know' Allah, and that His Command courses through the creation, and that His omnipotence and His omniscience envelop all things."

Commenting on the above verse, **Imam al-Sa'di** writes of the creation that, *"All of this was [created] in order for people to know and to discern that His knowledge and power circumscribe each and every thing. As they come to know Him through His Beautiful Names and Sublime Attributes, they will then adore and worship Him, and also fulfill His rights. This is the greater purpose behind the creation and command: to know Allah and to then worship Him."*

Ibn al-Qayyim has noted: *"In the Qur'an, Allah, Exalted is He, invites people to acquire ma'rifah; or knowledge and gnosis [of Him], via two ways: Firstly, by reflecting upon the divine handiwork [in creation]; and secondly, by contemplating over the Qur'an and pondering over its meanings. The former are His signs that are seen and witnessed, the latter are His signs which are heard and understood. The first type is referred to in His saying:* **In the creation of the heavens and the earth; in the alternation of the night and day; in the sailing of ships through the ocean for the benefit of mankind; in the water that Allah sends down from the sky and with which He revives the earth after its death; in the animals of all kinds that He has scattered therein; in the ordering of the winds and the clouds that are driven between heaven and earth, are signs for people who can think. (2:164)**

"And His words: **In the creation of the heavens and the earth, and in the alternation of the night and day, are signs for those of understanding. (3:190)**

"Verses like these occur frequently in the Qur'an. The second is referred to in His saying: **Will they not reflect on the Qur'an? (4:84)**

"As well as: **Do they not reflect about what is being said?** (23:68)

And: **This is a Book that We have sent down to you, full of blessings, that they may reflect over its signs.** (38:29)

Such verses also occur frequently."

In conclusion, we see that far from being an experiment or a form of amusement — God forbid! — the Almighty and Wise created us and this universe and all that is in it **so that we may know Him.**

May peace be with you,
Ahmed

Conversation with Denise

A Better Understanding in Forty-Two Questions

Email #02 – From: Denise
Sent: Tuesday, September 9, 2014 1:49 a.m.

Hello Ahmed,

Thank you for writing me. My name is Denise. I have heard many things about Islam, and I just wanted to know about it more in-depth. Before I ask these questions, I just want to let you know that I do not mean any harm. I do not mean to attack this belief; please do not interpret my questions this way. I just do not fully understand some concepts, and I am trying to gain a better understanding.

These questions may seem kind of randomly placed, so I will list them out.

1) If God sends prophets to all nations in their time of need, why is Muhammad the final prophet?

2) If God sent prophets to every nation, is there a reason why there is little record of monotheistic faiths in ancient times?

3) Is Islam monotheistic or henotheistic? Henotheistic means that other gods are recognized but you only worship/pray to one.

4) If Islam tries not to overly glorify the prophets, why is Muhammad so important? By this I mean, why is he the one mentioned in the *Shahada*?

5) If Islam does not see Jesus (Prophet Isa?) as the Son of God, why is he called the Messiah? What does the Qur'an say about the second coming?

5) I hear Muhammad preached about tolerance, so why did he destroy all of the idols that were in the Kaaba? (My account of the story may be wrong here.)

6) Were there women prophets?

7) What is the status of women in Islam?

8) I believe I heard once that the Bible is considered a holy book in Islam, but since it has been tampered and changed over the centuries, Muslims today use the Qur'an. Can there potentially be other holy books?

9) Why is it so bad to give God human characteristics?

I am sorry about the lengthy list of questions. I am looking forward to your response.

Thank you,
Denise

Email #03 – From: Ahmed Rashed
Sent: Thursday, September 11, 2014 9:27 a.m.

In the Name of God; Most Gracious, Most Merciful:

Hello Denise,

These are very good questions, so we'll reply to each separately.

1. First of all, the premise of your question is not true. Islam does not teach that "God sends prophets to all nations in their time of need." Rather it teaches that a prophet is sent for two reasons: first, if a community has never received any messenger. Second, if the teachings of a previous messenger have been lost, abandoned, or changed, a new messenger is sent to correct them. Also, remember that the mission of each individual prophet was not the same. Every prophet was sent to his immediate community only. Every messenger was sent to his immediate community and the communities surrounding them. Only the Final Messenger was sent to his immediate community and all communities of mankind present and future. As long as the revelation of God and the teachings of a messenger are intact, God does not send a new prophet. Since all previous prophets and messengers have had their teachings or scriptures lost, abandoned, or changed, and since the Prophet Muhammad's (peace be upon him) teachings and scripture are still intact, there is no need for any new prophet.

2. The Islamic worldview, like the Christian and Jewish worldview, is that monotheism was the original religion of humanity but was generally lost after people went astray from prophetic teachings. As for the idea that there is little record of monotheistic faith in ancient times, most scholars point to the scarcity of writing as the reason. If a society and culture is

primarily propagated by art, poetry, and storytelling, it is reasonable to conclude that these more fluid forms of communication would more easily lose any monotheistic center. There is recent scholarship that showcases traces of monotheism in ancient cultures. See the following links:

http://www.usu.edu/markdamen/1320hist&Civ/chapters/10AKHEN.htm

http://www.submission.info/perspectives/monotheism/monotheism_since_ancient_times.html

3. Islam is monotheistic; the creed and central tenant of Islam is "There IS NO God but God."

4. First of all, Muhammad (pbuh) is not the most frequently mentioned in the Qur'an. Rather, that honor goes to Prophet Moses (pbuh), Prophet Jesus (pbuh), and Prophet Noah (pbuh), who are mentioned 136, 59, and 43 times respectively. As for why Muhammad (pbuh) is in the Shahadah, this is because believing in Muhammad's (pbuh) message means you accept all previous prophets and messengers.

5. The reason is because the Kaaba is believed to have been built by Prophets Abraham (pbuh) and Ishamael (pbuh) for the worship of God. By the time of Muhammad (pbuh), that temple of monotheism had been contaminated by idolatry. One of Muhammad's (pbuh) tasks was to cleanse and sanctify that original house of worship to be for God alone.

6. No, there were no women prophets. That is because prophets are expected to be rejected, ridiculed, persecuted, and maybe even tortured or abused for their preaching. Out of God's mercy, and to maintain the honor and integrity of prophethood, this difficult burden has only been commissioned to men.

7. Prophet Muhammad (pbuh) said, "Women are the twin halves of men." The Qur'an holds that women are independent agents, accountable for their own deeds, whether good or bad. They have the same responsibilities to worship God and obey His commandments. Islam revolutionized society by elevating the status of women. Islam granted women rights to contract, to work and earn money, to inherit, and to own property independently of

men. Wives keep their identity and are not expected to adopt their husband's name. Islam also stipulates rights for their education, maintenance, inheritance, and protection — rights that were not present in the pre-Islamic period.

While a gap exists between the rights of women outlined in the Qur'an and the prevalent reality in the Muslim world, the overall concept in Islam is one of allowing and expecting women to be major contributors to the development of a healthy and productive society. The main complaint against Islam regarding women is the dress code that Islam stipulates for observant women. This dress code is actually not too different from the dress code that Islam mandates for men, but today's society exploits women's sexuality more than men's sexuality, so the Islamic dress code is more noticeable for women. The small difference between men and women's dress code is merely a reflection of the difference between men and women's bodies and the difference between what triggers temptation in men and women's minds.

8. There are five scriptures mentioned by name in the Qur'an: the Scrolls of Abraham, the Torah of Moses, the Psalms of David, the Evangel of Jesus, and the Qur'an of Muhammad. However, Prophet Muhammad (pbuh) said that over one hundred scriptures have been revealed by God since the descent of Adam. None of the scriptures except the Qur'an is still as it was when first revealed.

9. One of the primary reasons for God sending prophets and messengers and scriptures in the first place is so mankind would achieve Gnosis, or in Arabic "ma'rifat Allah" or "knowing God." This means knowing who God is and what attributes and names He has, and more importantly, what attributes he DOES NOT have. Although we can understand some of His attributes, His essence cannot be comprehended by a human's limited mental capacity. God has created mankind primarily so that they may know their Creator through His creations. More directly to your question, attributing human characteristics to God necessarily implies attributing human frailty and/or shortcomings, but this is exactly the opposite of what Islam came to preach!

The attributes of Almighty God preclude any evil, since God is the source of justice, mercy, and truth. God can never be thought of as doing an ungodly act. Hence we cannot imagine God telling a lie, being unjust, making a mistake, forgetting things, or having any such human failings. Similarly, God can do injustice if He chooses to, but He will never do it, because being unjust is an ungodly act.

See this link for further discussion of consequences of attributing human-like attributes and shortcomings to our Creator:

http://www.suhaibwebb.com/personaldvlpt/character/thinking-well-of-allah/

I hope this addressed your questions. Feel free to follow up if you have more questions or would like to further discuss these answers.

May peace be with you,
Ahmed

Email #04 – From: Denise
Sent: Tuesday, September 16, 2014 11:17 p.m.

Hello Ahmed,

Thank you for answering these questions, but of course I now have more. Some of them are related to the ones I asked previously, and some of them are not.

1) What does Islam say about the rights of animals? Do they have souls? Are humans superior to them?

2) If God needs no helpers, what are the angels for? What is their role?

3) Can you explain the Islamic viewpoint of Gnosis? I only have knowledge of it from a Christian viewpoint. The one in which Gnosticism was the rival sect when the official Catholic Church was established. Is the Gnostic viewpoint of Islam similar to Sufism?

4) Is it true that Muhammad killed people? I believe it was during a time of war, but does this serve some sort of purpose?

5) I have heard that Islam is not supposed to be divided into different sects, but is there a certain sect that remains true to Muhammad's revelations?

6) What do you think are the most common misconceptions about Islam?

7) Why did God only create humans to worship him?

8) Why did God tell the angels to bow down before Adam? Why did Shaytan get punished for refusing?

Thank you for taking the time to answer these questions,
Denise

Email #05 – From: Ahmed Rashed
Sent: Tuesday, September 23, 2014 9:26 a.m.

In the Name of God; Most Gracious, Most Merciful:

Hello Denise,

We are always happy to answer your questions; that is what we are here for. Regarding your questions:

1. Animals have rights as any other creation of God. The Prophet (pbuh) forbade neglecting of pets (cats/dogs) and beating of mounts (horses, camels, mules). Also, the Prophet mentioned that even the ewe that was pushed by a ram would appear on the Day of Judgment to have her injustice reckoned, so yes, they have souls. As for superiority, the Qur'an says: **We have honored the Children of Adam ... and conferred on them special bounty above most of Creation. (17:70)**

2. Angels are executors of God's commands, but their primary purpose is worshiping and glorifying God. So there are angels of revelation who communicate His wishes to the prophets. There are angels of rain and angels of recording deeds and angels who take the souls of the deceased and so on. Yes, God does not "need" any of these servants, but angels are created not for the purpose of helping God but for worshiping him. They are entrusted with applying the laws of God in the universe. This is their worship, and this is how they glorify His Name.

However, while angels reflect the perfect names and attributes of God, mankind was created so there would be a creature that could CHOOSE to contemplate, understand, appreciate, and live up to the Divine Names.

3. Gnosis, or Intimate Knowledge of God, is related to the previous question in that it is the primary reason why God created sentient beings; especially sentient beings who have the free will to obey or disobey Him. The understanding of the Divine Names and Attributes is what sets apart the free-willed from the rest of Creation. A human being who observes mercy in his life, then contemplates how this observed mercy is but a small portion of the vast reserve of divine mercy, and appreciates this bounty and then turns to the source of this bounty, has recognized God in a way that creatures lacking free will could never achieve. Likewise, Sufi orders historically focused on these Divine Names such as the *Forgiver*, the *Pardoner*, the *Powerful*, the *Sublime*, etc., to lift up their followers to a spiritual awakening to complement the ritual observances. However, even orthodox non-Sufi interpretations of Islam highlight the importance of seeking God, and by seeking God, knowing God, and from knowing God, serving and worshiping God.

4. Muhammad (pbuh) only killed one person with his own hands, and that was during the Battle of Uhud. However, it is true that he commanded armies where his soldiers fought and killed the enemy, and he was the leader of a state that enforced capital punishment on murderers and similar criminals. This is understood in the context of the Qur'an, **"and do not kill the soul which God has made sacred, except for justice." (6:151)**

The meaning of "except for justice" is explained by all the modern and traditional scholars as meaning a) self-defense in the face of imminent death, b) Punishment for capital crime, or c) killing an enemy soldier on the battlefield during war. These are the regulations that the Qur'an and Islam lay down for when it is permissible to take life. In any other condition, the taking of life is considered a sin and a crime.

5. Anyone who follows the teachings of the Qur'an and the Traditions of the Prophet and the mainstream understanding of those teachings are considered to be on the right path. This is what is meant by *Ahl as-Sunnah wa Jama'ah*: the People of Tradition and Consensus.

6. The most common misconception is that Islam teaches its followers to hate, fight, and kill non-Muslims. On the contrary, the Qur'an enjoins its followers to be just, even if there is animosity between you and another party. Also the Qur'an (60:8-9) clearly outlines that the only conditions for fighting are against those who fight you because of your faith or try to drive you out of your homes.

7. See answer to 2 and 3

8. This requires a bit of backstory: the understanding is that before the creation of man, there were jinn on the Earth, and they were the Keepers of God's Covenant. After their term came to an end, the best of the jinn, named Iblis, was allowed to dwell in Paradise with God's angels. When God created Adam, it was then that he commanded all in Paradise to bow to Adam out of respect and humility for God's handiwork. All the angels did so because angels have no free will; they cannot disobey God's commands. However, the Qu'ran (8:50) states that Iblis **"was one of the jinn, and he broke the command his Lord."**

Now as for why was Iblis punished for disobeying God, you have to remember that any act of disobedience to God's command is a sin, and all sins are due for punishment. This is a manifestation of God's Names the *Just*, the *Avenger*, the *All-Mighty*, and the *Reckoner*. The only thing that stays punishment is either repentance from the sinner or pardon from the Creator. Notice that in the Qur'anic version of the creation story, Adam and Eve feel remorse and regret and ask God for forgiveness and are then forgiven, so no punishment befalls them (in contrast to Christian understanding). However, Iblis (Satan) did not repent or regret, and therefore his deserved punishment was not abated; it was merely delayed to the Day of Judgment.

Good questions!

Looking forward to hearing from you soon.
May peace be with you,
Ahmed

Email #06 – From: Denise
Sent: Saturday, October 4, 2014 12:48 a.m.

Hello Ahmed,
Asalam Alaykum.

Thank you for answering these questions. Your answers have been helping my understanding of Islam. I now have more questions.

1. Is it necessary for Muslims to sacrifice a sheep on Eid al-Adha? Can something else be sacrificed? Does an animal really need to be slaughtered?

2. Do you know anything about Islamic mysticism?

3. Are there any Islamic saints?

4. If the Qur'an allows killing "for justice," does Islam politically promote capital punishment? What is the capital crime?

5. Do non-Muslims go to "hell"?

6. Is there an angelic hierarchy according to Islam?

7. According to Islam, are there other beings beside angels, jinns, and humans (including all of the creatures on Earth)?

8. Is there a possibility in Islam that Jesus was crucified?

9. Is reincarnation possible in Islam?

Thank you for everything.
-Denise

Email #07 – From: Ahmed Rashed
Sent: Friday, October 10, 2014 8:51 a.m.

In the Name of God; Most Gracious, Most Merciful:

Assalaamu alaikum, Denise:

1. A Muslim may sacrifice one sheep or goat. Alternatively, seven Muslims may share in sacrificing one cow or camel. Sacrificing an animal is a requirement, as it represents the sacrifice

Abraham (pbuh) made in place of his son. It is a show of obedience to God and an offering of thanks and a method to feed poor people.

2. As for Islamic mysticism, I know little. The Sufi paths started out as a reaction to the eighth and ninth century trends towards the overly legalistic expression of Islamic philosophy. They emphasize *dhikr* (remembrance) of God and the ascetic way of life. Most Sufi teachings are in line with the Qur'an and the Sunnah of the Prophet, but a few have deviated from those teachings.

3. Saints as understood in the Christian world do not have parallels in the Islamic world. That is because no human being is infallible. Even prophets and messengers, according to the teachings of Islam, are only infallible when it comes to the revelation of God's religion and the application of God's religion. In purely worldly matters, they can make mistakes like anyone else. The closest thing to a saint is Islam is the "*Wali*" or "Beloved" of God. This is a person who has high personal piety and through this constant remembrance of God attains what the Prophet mentioned in the following Hadith Qudsi: *"Allah the Almighty has said, 'Nothing endears My servant to Me more than doing of what I have made obligatory upon him to do. And My servant continues to draw nearer to Me with extra devotions so that I shall love him. When I love him, I shall be his hearing with which he shall hear, his sight with which he shall see, his hands with which he shall hold, and his feet with which he shall walk. And if he asks of Me, I shall surely give it to him, and if he takes refuge in Me, I shall certainly grant him it.'"* (Bukhari)

4. Since Islam is a complete way of life, it offers instruction on crime and punishment. Islam on the whole accepts capital punishment. But even though the death penalty is allowed, forgiveness is preferable. Forgiveness, together with peace, is a predominant Qur'an theme. In Islamic law, the death penalty is appropriate for two groups of crimes:

a) Intentional murder: In these cases the victim's family is given the option as to whether to insist on execution of the murderer or to forgive.

b) *Fasad fil-ardh* (spreading mischief in the land): Islam permits the death penalty for those who threaten public safety. What constitutes the crime of "spreading mischief in the land" is open to interpretation, but the following crimes are usually included: treason, rape, public adultery, armed robbery, and similar aggressions.

5. The question of who goes to Hell can only be answered by God Himself. Except for the few personalities that have been explicitly named as inhabitants of Hell in the Qur'an or authentic sayings of the Prophet, no one can say whether anyone, Muslim or not Muslim, will for certain enter Hell. Now, the understanding from the Qur'an is that God never punishes a person or community until He sends them a messenger (17:15). This messenger does NOT have to be a prophet. It means any person with comprehensive knowledge who has engaged the recipient with wisdom. Imam Al-Ghazali talks about three groups of non-Muslims: one group who has never even heard the name Muhammad, one group who has heard of Muhammad but never any accurate information about him or Islam (only misconceptions, lies, slander, etc.), and one group who heard the message of Muhammad and Islam, understood it, had all misconceptions clarified, but still chose not to accept Islam. Only the third group is called a "disbeliever," because only the third group actually understood the message to be disbelieved! The first two are excused and will be sent a messenger on the Day of Judgment as a test. Those who pass the test and believe shall enter Paradise, but those who fail the test and disbelieve will enter Hell.

6. As for angelic hierarchy in Islam, there are only general organizational themes, not actual classes or ranks. You can check out the following links:
http://www.archangels-and-angels.com/misc/angels_islam.html
http://angels.about.com/od/AngelBasics/f/What-Are-Angel-Types-In-Islam.htm

7. The only sentient beings mentioned by name in the Qur'an are angels, jinn, and humans. It is possible there are other beings, because the Qur'an says in many places that "**all who are**

in the heavens and earth glorify God," so this could mean the aforementioned three beings or it could allude to others. The Qur'an also states that **"God creates what He wishes"** and **"God increases His creation as He wishes,"** so the door is open to other sentient beings existing, but the Qur'an and Hadith only mention those three.

8. No. The Qur'an clearly states: **And for their saying, "We have killed the Messiah, Jesus, the son of Mary, the Messenger of God." In fact, they did not kill him, nor did they crucify him, but it appeared to them as if they did. Indeed, those who differ about him are in doubt about it. They have no knowledge of it, except the following of assumptions. Certainly, they did not kill him. Rather, God raised him up to Himself. God is Mighty and Wise. There is none from the People of the Scripture but will believe in him before his death, and on the Day of Resurrection he will be a witness against them. (4:157-159)**

9. No, the Qur'an clearly states that all souls will taste death, and they will taste it only once after living. We start dead (non-existence), then we are given life, then we die (normal death), then we are resurrected, then we face God on Judgment Day: **How can you reject Allah, when you were dead and then He gave you life, then He will make you die and then give you life again, then you will be returned to Him? (2:28)**

> May peace be with you,
> Ahmed

Email #08 – From: Denise
Sent: Friday, November 14, 2014 12:42 a.m.

> Hello Ahmed,
> Thank you for answering those questions. I am very sorry it has taken me such a long time to respond. I have more questions.
> 1) If the Qur'an is the word of God, why do Muslims refer to the Hadith a lot?

2) Can women be imams? Why or why not?

3) What is a sheik? (I may be using the wrong word).

4) Why did Muhammad preach against monastic life?

5) What is the purpose of an imam vs. a priest?

6) Would it be allowable for a Muslim to not take the Qur'an 100% literally?

7) Why don't Muslims believe in the concept of original sin?

8) What is the point/purpose of the ninety-nine names of God?

9) Why is homosexuality not allowed?

10) Do humans have free will, or does God decide our every action?

Thank you very much.

Email #09 – From: Ahmed Rashed
Sent: Monday, November 24, 2014 2:02 p.m.

In the Name of God; Most Gracious, Most Merciful:

Good morning Denise,

No need to apologize for taking long to respond. We are all busy in this hectic thing we call life, so such delays are expected. Let us get right to your questions.

Muslims refer to the Hadith because every scripture that God has ever revealed has always come with a messenger to explain and teach how to implement it. If scripture was sufficient, God would not have any need to commission prophets or messengers. He would simply etch his words on a mountain or tablet of steel, and all who wanted divine guidance could just look it up. But scripture has always been revealed to a human messenger so that people would have a mentor and role model on how to implement the general principles that God revealed in His Words. The Qur'an is no different. So just as the Qur'an commands us to be good to parents, to give charity, and to pray, it is the Hadith (sayings and actions of the Prophet) that show us HOW to fulfill these commandments.

As for female imams, women are allowed to be imams when leading the prayer for a group of women. They are also allowed to be teachers and scholars and advisers, whether the students/seekers are male or female. However, if there is a mixed group of men and women who want to perform one of the five daily prayers, only a man can be imam in that case. The reason for this is the same reason why women and men are separated during these ritual prayers: the movements of the prayer preclude women standing in front of men for modesty. Since these prayers involve bowing and prostrating, it is immodest for a woman to do perform these actions in front of men. So women pray behind men or off to the side of the mosque or in a separate room.

For this reason, you will see male imams referred to as *sheikh* and female imams referred to as *sheikha*. The title literally means "elder" and is an honorific implying knowledge and wisdom. Basically, anyone who has a strong religious knowledge base is called *sheikh* or *sheikha*, even if they do not lead any prayers or give any classes. Note that this is a generic meaning. Some Sufi orders use the title *sheikh* to specifically identify the founder or spiritual leader of their order.

In terms of spirituality, the Prophet Muhammad (pbuh) taught moderation and balance in all acts. So indulging in food, sex, and merriment in a hedonistic way was condemned. Abstaining from food, sex, and merriment was also condemned. Both are considered extremes against the idea of living a fulfilling but God-conscious life. The Prophet taught us that we were not created except to worship God, but that worship is by acknowledging His Beneficence and enjoying His bounties in a lawful, ethical way. For this reason, monasticism is not encouraged. A human being is supposed to be a steward on Earth, which means getting involved in establishing justice and striving to cultivate the Earth according to God's guidelines. Running away from the worldly life is directly opposite to this purpose.

So an imam's role is to lead the obligatory prayers. This is the minimum definition and purpose, and it is usually what is meant when we say "This person is the imam of that mosque."

Imams can also be mentors, teachers, scholars, and counselors; however, unlike a priest, this is not a requirement. Also, an imam is not an acquired title, like priest. No one can "ordain" an imam. It is an honorific title first and a designated title only if the personal qualifications of the person warrant it.

As for the literalness of the Qur'an, most scholars would say no. The Qur'an is accepted to be the literal Word of God. The only flexibility in interpretation is for those verses that have multiple linguistic meanings and for which there is no explicit explanation from the Prophet himself. Since the texts of the Qur'an and the Hadith are so well-preserved, very few verses of the Qur'an would allow for anything other than a literal acceptance. This is because historically, for other scriptures, the authenticity and integrity of the text itself is an open question, so scholars of the Bible have the liberty to question whether a certain verse was ACTUALLY proclaimed by Moses, David, Jesus, etc. Also, since there are a few instances of verses being in direct contradiction to known historical or scientific facts or in contradiction to other verses, the necessity of critiquing the Bible became manifest. The Qur'an actually has no internal contradictions, and even more amazingly, there are no verses that literally contradict science or history. Even those verses that Orientalists have pointed out as being incompatible with Biblical accounts of a story (such as the story of Pharaoh) or with science (such as the expanding heavens), the Qur'an has eventually proven to be true. This vindication is what makes Muslims so confident in the future predictions of the Qur'an: if all these stories and descriptions of nature have been confirmed to be true, then the likelihood that these predictions or descriptions that cannot be confirmed yet are probably also true.

Original sin is a concept that is only acceptable if you believe the premise that God is "so holy" that He cannot forgive Adam's sin. The Qur'an does not deny that Adam and Eve disobeyed God; it only denies that God was unable or unwilling to simply forgive them.

In the biblical account, Adam and Eve fall from Paradise as a result of disobeying God's prohibition, and all of humanity is cast out of Paradise as punishment. Based upon this reading of the story, Christian theologians developed the doctrine that humankind is born with this sin of their first parents still on their souls. Most Christians believe Jesus Christ came to redeem humans from this original sin so they can return to God at the end of time.

In contrast, the Qur'an states that after their initial disobedience, Adam and Eve repented and were forgiven by God. Because of this, Muslims believe all humans are born free of any stigma or sin. The descent of Adam and Eve to Earth from Paradise is not seen as a fall, but as an honor bestowed on them by God. Adam and his progeny were appointed as God's stewards and were entrusted by God with the guardianship of the Earth.

The ninety-nine names or attributes of God are merely linguistic descriptions of Our Creator so the human being can know God, and from knowing God, appreciate and LOVE God. There are more than just ninety-nine, of course; but the saying of the Prophet mentions ninety-nine as a way to show how completely God manifests Himself to His creation.

Homosexuality is considered like any other form of excess: it is a form of pleasure that is outside of the boundaries that God has set forth for a Godly way of life. Like many other lifestyle choices, God has explained in His books and through His prophets that sexuality is a part of human nature that should be regulated and balanced like food, drink, and entertainment. The "why" is because God said so; the "wisdom" behind that commandment is subject to human debate and conjecture, but it does not invalidate the reason for the commandment or the validity of that commandment.

Humans have free will. Otherwise, it would be a joke to reward the righteous and injustice to punish the wicked. Just because God knows what you will choose does not mean he has coerced you into making your choices.

May peace be with you,
Ahmed

Email #10 – From: Denise
Sent: Friday, February 6, 2015 12:01 a.m.

Hello Ahmed,

Peace be with you. Thank you for answering my questions. Your answers are very helpful. I am sorry that it has taken me so long to respond.

1) If Islam is supposed to be unified, why are there so many sects?

2) I have been trying to read the Qur'an, but I am one of those people who have a hard time concentrating when reading. Do you have any suggestions to overcome this? Are there any passages that I should read first? Or should I read them in order?

3) I am not sure if you know the Christian versions of the stories, but how are Moses's, Jesus's, and Noah's stories different from the Bible to the Qur'an?

4) Do Muslims believe in the second coming of Jesus? If they do, is it like the Catholic concept of establishing God's kingdom on Earth?

5) Is going to Friday (jummah?) prayer on Fridays required? Is it considered a sin not to attend like if a Christian does not attend church on Sunday?

6) Is vegetarianism/veganism acceptable in Islam?

Thank you again for being so helpful!
-Denise

Email #11 – From: Ahmed Rashed
Sent: Friday, February 20, 2015 4:25 p.m.

In the Name of God; Most Gracious, Most Merciful:

Hello Denise,

There is One Islam but Many Muslims. There is no pope or official hierarchy in Islam, so only the consensus of the scholars has any binding weight. Also, there is a well-known Saying of the Prophet (peace be upon him): "My community will divide into seventy-three groups. All of them are in the Fire except one." When asked which one is the saved group, he replied, "That which I and my Companions are upon."

More importantly, Islam is a journey, not a destination. The test of this life, as the Qur'an mentions time and time again, is to see who will be the best of deeds and character. Who will emulate the Prophet and live a God-conscious life dedicated to serving God and God's creatures, establishing justice, and striving against all forms of oppression. So some people will do this and some people will not. Also, as we see in this day and age, some people will act in a way repugnant to the teachings of the Prophet (pbuh) and claim that they are doing it in his name, in God's name, or in Islam's name.

As for reading the Qur'an, personally I have seen some people read from beginning to end without issue. I've seen others who get confused this way so they read from end to beginning. It really depends on the person. Two of my students started at the beginning and would email me after each page to ask questions or get commentary so they'd understand the meaning and context of the passage they just read. You could do that too, if you want; it would be an honor to help you understand the Book of God.

On the other hand, what I do in my "Living Islam" class is start in the middle of the Qur'an (Sura 29, to be exact) and read to the end of the Qur'an, and THEN start from the beginning again. This has been well-received so far, so you could try that too.

The stories of Moses (pbuh) are mostly compatible, although the Qur'an does not relate all the episodes that are mentioned in the Bible. As for Jesus (pbuh), the primary difference is the emphasis on his humanity and lack of divine status. The story of Noah (pbuh) is also mostly compatible, although some scholars point out that the flood as described in the Qur'an was a localized flood of Noah's valley, not an Earth-spanning deluge.

As for the second coming of Christ, yes, the Prophet (pbuh) explicitly taught his Companions that the Son of Mary would return to the Earth and establish justice. He would join the Muslims and fight against the Anti-Christ. Then he would marry, live a normal life as ruler, and die a natural death.

The Friday sermon and prayer is obligatory for men, but it is not obligatory for women, children, the very ill, or those who are travelers. Obviously, if one of the secondary group chooses to go, it is a virtuous good deed on their record. If a healthy resident man does not go to Friday prayer, then it is considered a sin unless there is some constraining reason.

As for the vegetarian or vegan diet, there is nothing per se against abstaining from meat or animal products. However, there are some acts of worship (end of Hajj, for example, or the new baby celebration) that require the slaughter or sacrifice of an animal. So the vegan or vegetarian worldview that animals should not be slaughtered for consumption is against the Qur'anic verses that mention these animals as placed on Earth by God for man to use and consume so long as it is in a merciful way. For example, there are verses that talk about distributing meat to the poor and others that talk how the fur, skin, and meat of animals are for people to use. On the other hand, the Prophet forbade cruelty to animals, so even when slaughtering, there are etiquettes to prevent alarm or excessive pain in the animal.

May peace be with you,
Ahmed

Conversation with Roger

The Islam and Peace Debate

Email #02 – From: Roger
Sent: Tuesday, August 28, 2015 10:21 p.m.

Ahmed, thanks for the reply. The real basis of my inquiries is this: When defining peace and Islam, how are we defining it? Why are there peaceful texts followed later by seemingly unpeaceful texts?

We have peaceful texts:
The [Muslim] believers, the Jews, the Christians, and the Sabians — all those who believe in God and the Last Day and do good — will have their rewards with their Lord. No fear for them, nor will they grieve. (2:62)

None of you will attain true piety unless you give out of what you cherish: whatever you give, God knows about it very well. (3:92)

[O Prophet,] You are sure to find that the most hostile to the believers are the Jews and those who associate other deities with God; you are sure to find that the closest in affection towards the believers are those who say, 'We are Christians,' for there are among them people devoted to learning and ascetics. These people are not given to arrogance. (5:82)

Another of His signs is that He created spouses from among yourselves for you to live with in tranquillity: He ordained love and kindness between you. There truly are signs in this for those who reflect. (30:21)

And non-peaceful texts:
You who believe, do not take the Jews and Christians as allies: they are allies only to each other. Anyone who takes them as an ally becomes one of them — God does not guide such wrongdoers. (5:51)

Your Lord revealed to the angels: 'I am with you: give the believers firmness; I shall put terror into the hearts of the disbelievers — strike above their necks and strike all their fingertips.' (8:12)

When the forbidden months are over, wherever you encounter the idolaters, kill them, seize them, besiege them, wait for them at every lookout post; but if they repent, maintain the prayer, and pay the prescribed alms, let them go on their way, for God is most forgiving and merciful. (9:5)

Fight those of the People of the Book who do not believe in God and the Last Day, who do not forbid what God and His Messenger have forbidden, who do not obey the rule of justice, until they pay the *jizya* and agree to submit. (9:29)

Those who disbelieve among the People of the Book and the idolaters will have the Fire of Hell, there to remain. They are the worst of creation. (98:6)

How are we to decipher what suras to follow, peaceful or otherwise? Are Muslims, as interpreted in the Qur'an, to be friends of Christians and Jews?

Email #03 – From: Ahmed Rashed
Sent: Thursday, September 3, 2015 10:36 a.m.

In the Name of God; Most Gracious, Most Merciful

Good Morning, Roger:

I pray this email finds you in the best of health and faith, God willing. First of all, let me say that your questions are quite common, so please feel free to continue questioning until all concepts are clearly understood. I apologize that my response below is so long, but this is a very important topic in understanding the Qur'an, so I put a few examples to make it easier for you to understand, God willing.

Now let us address your point regarding verses about war and peace. You have to understand that the revelations of the Qur'an came down in a period of twenty-three years. The Prophet experienced many different situations in those twenty-three years, and the Qur'an was revealed in the context of those situations. You can almost think of them as a series of "letters" or "dictations" from God to Muhammad via the Archangel Gabriel. So in the beginning, God is telling Muhammad about Himself, His existence, power, and mercy. Also teaching Muhammad about the prophets and that Muhammad is one of those noble messengers. Also teaching Muhammad about the Day of Judgment and that it is coming and that human beings should prepare for that meeting with their Creator. As the Prophet invites his community to worship God and God alone, he encounters resistance, persecution, and hardships. God responds with lessons on humility, reminders of the final reward in Paradise for this work and for following this path, warnings against being heedless of this message, and stories of previous prophets and believers to soothe the Prophet and his followers in the face of all the hardships they are enduring for God's Cause.

Then, finally, the Prophet and his followers migrate to Medina. Now the yoke of persecution is lifted. Muslims can practice and preach without fear of retribution. Now, after thirteen years of emphasizing God and the Meeting with Him, the followers are ready for "How to Live a Godly Life?" So now God starts sending down instructions on morals, ethics, and behavior norms. Also, as the Meccans start threatening the very lives of all who follow Muhammad, God grants the Muslims permission to bear arms, to fight and defend themselves until they are able to practice and preach God's message.

So the concept of "which verses replace others" is not as clear cut. Some scholars only cite five verses what were abrogated by later verses, while some scholars cite over ninety verses that were abrogated. The majority claim that only ten to twelve verses were actually completely abrogated and the rest were "specifications" instead of outright "replacements." The most famous example of this is the explicit prohibition on wine. This prohibition was revealed in several stages to make it easier for the wine-loving Arabs to give up this destructive vice.

Stage 1 -*Declaring the moral status of wine*: **They ask you about wine and gambling. Say: "In them there is great sin, and some benefit for men; but the sin is greater than the benefit." (2:219)**

Stage 2 -*Restricting consumption of wine*: **O Believers! Do not approach prayers when drunk until you know what you say, (4:43)**

Stage 3 -*Commanding the avoidance of wine*: **O Believers! Wine and gambling, idols and divining arrows are abominations of the Devil — shun them so that you may prosper. The Devil seeks to cause enmity and hatred among you by means of wine and gambling, and to keep you from the remembrance of God and your prayers. Will you not then abstain? (5:90-91)**

The latter of these verses technically do not "replace" the previous ones. They make more and more specific instructions. However, while these are not technical replacements, they ARE a more developed meaning. No one now would try to argue that it is sufficient for Muslims to simply avoid being drunk during prayer. The Muslim community is now past that phase, and it is expected all observant Muslims will totally abstain from drinking.

Another example is the infamous Verse of the Sword **(9:5)** that many Islam-haters use to show that Muslims are not allowed to be nice or peaceful with non-Muslims. That is simply not true. First, looking at the immediate context, we see that verse 13 of the same chapter mentions a few reasons for this particular war declaration. This verse mentions people who initiated hostilities, who drove the Prophet and the believers out of their homes, and who then broke their peace agreements (referring to the Treaty of Hudaybiyah). In addition, verses 8 and 10 condemn them because they totally disregarded ties of kinship and treaties.

It's clear here that Islam is not waging war against all pagans or all non-believers. It is clear that the Prophet did not historically understand this verse to mean the killing of all pagans. For example, when the conquest of Mecca took place, the Prophet issued a general pardon to all its inhabitants, who were not only pagans but also those that had fought him for the longest time, and regarding whom many of those verses had been revealed. More importantly, it is clear that these verses don't "replace" the previous verses that talk about being just and kind to people in general. So it is not the case that the Qur'an "used to" preach peace and tolerance and then "in the end" advocated stern warfare. Rather, the context of the peace and tolerance verses are the general normative teachings, and the stern warfare verses are the specific situation of dealing with a group who are threatening your very existence.

I hope this addressed your concerns. Feel free to reply with any further questions or clarifications.

May peace be with you,
Ahmed

Email #04 – From: Roger
Sent: Sunday, September 6, 2015 12:31 p.m.

Ahmed, thanks so much for answering my questions,

My first question has to do with what you said, *"the context of the peace and tolerance verses are the general normative teachings and the stern warfare verses are the specific situation of dealing with a group who are threatening your very existence."* If this is really the case, then why the hostile words for Christians who did not threaten Muslims during Muhammad's time? In fact Muhammad sent his people to Christians, and Christians openly protected Muslims during Muhammad's life (Ethopia). What are the circumstances for Sura 98.6, 5:51, 9.29 and others like it that are openly hostile to Christians?

My second question has to do with the issues that arise when there are no clear specifics in interpretation of peace or otherwise. Like you said, one sura does not abrogate the other; they coexist, so this means that the nonviolent and violent interpretations are equally valid. Can the claim that Islam is a peaceful religion be made if there are clearly non-peaceful texts?

Email #05 – From: Ahmed Rashed
Sent: Monday, September 14, 2015 11:20 a.m.

In the Name of God; Most Gracious, Most Merciful:

Good morning, Roger:

I apologize for not getting back to you last week. It was very busy at work, and my mother had an operation, so my availability was not what it usually is. Rest assured there is no difficulty in answering your questions, my friend; it is merely finding time to sit down and type them out. Remember, we are volunteers. To get to your points, here are the contexts for the verses you cited:

98:6 - First of all, this verse is not statement of hostility to Christians. Rather it is explaining the need of sending a messenger and what the consequences of rejecting that messenger and his message will be. It says that the people of the world, be they from among the followers of the earlier scriptures or from among the idolaters, could not possibly be freed from their state of incorrect belief until a messenger was sent. Also, he should present the Book of God before the people in its original, pristine form, which should be free from every mixture of falsehood corrupting the earlier divine books, and which should comprise sound teachings.

Then, about the errors of the followers of the earlier books, it states that the cause of their straying into different creeds was not that God had not provided any guidance to them, but they strayed only after a clear statement of the Right Creed had come to them. From this it automatically follows that they themselves were responsible for their error and deviation. Now, if even after the coming of the clear statement through this Messenger, they continued to stray, their responsibility would further increase. That is the meaning of 98:6, that the message of the final messenger is obligated on all those who receive it, whether pagan, Jew, Christian, or otherwise.

The Qur'an teaches that all the prophets enjoined the path of sincere and true service to the Creator. This has been the true religion from the start. From this, it automatically follows that the followers of the earlier scriptures, straying from this true religion, have added extraneous things to it. Therefor, this messenger has come from God to invite them back to the same original faith.

5:51 - This verse must be read with the next two verses to be understood. This passage refers to the condition of the hypocrites during the period when the conflict between Muslims and pagans had not yet come to any decisive conclusion. In his Qur'an commentary, Imam Ibn Kathir has mentioned that some scholars say this verse was revealed after the Battle of Uhud when Muslims suffered a major loss. At that time, a Muslim from Madinah said, "I am going to live with the Jews so I shall be safe in case another attack comes on Medina." And another person said, "I am going to live with the Christians so I shall be safe in case another attack comes on Medina." So God revealed this verse reminding the believers that they should not seek the protection from others but should protect each other. (See Ibn Kathir, Al-Tafsir, vol. 2, p. 68)

As an aside, Muslims are allowed to have non-Muslims as friends as long as they are able to keep their own faith and commitment to Islam pure and strong. Notice that a Muslim man is also allowed to marry a Jewish or Christian woman. It is obvious that one marries someone for love and friendship. If friendship between Muslims and Jews or Christians was forbidden, then why would Islam allow a Muslim man to marry a Jew or Christian woman?

Back to our topic: this verse is not about "friends" but rather "allies" or "patrons," which is a more proper translation of the Arabic word *awliyaa*. The verse is saying that it is the duty of Muslims to patronize Muslims. They should not patronize anyone who is against their faith or who fights their faith, even if they were their fathers and brothers.

The Qur'an says: **O you who believe! Take not for protectors (*awliyaa*) your fathers and your brothers if they love unbelief above faith. If any of you do so, they are indeed wrong-doers. (9:23)**

In a similar way, if some Muslims do wrong to some non-Muslims, it is the Muslim's duty to help the non-Muslims and save them from oppression. The Prophet (peace and blessings be upon him) said that he himself will defend a non-Muslim living among Muslims to whom injustice is done by Muslims. Islam does teach that Muslims should not seek the patronage of non-Muslims against other Muslims, but this is understood to mean Muslim polities should try to solve their problems among themselves: **Let not the Believers take the unbelievers as their patrons (*awliyaa*) against the Believers. (3:28)**

O you who believe! Take not for patrons (*awliyaa*) unbelievers rather than Believers. Do you wish to offer God an open proof against yourselves? (4:144)

9:29 - This verse is about tax evasion and treason, my friend. The command to fight in this verse is conditional "until they pay the *jizya*," which is the tax levied on non-Muslim MEN of military age and ability. Slaves, women, children, the old, the sick, monks, hermits and the poor, were all exempt from the tax. *Jizya* was levied in the time of Muhammad on vassal tribes under Muslim control and protection, including the Jews in Khaybar, the Christians in Najran, and the Zoroastrians in Bahrain.

In addition, there were communities who chose to fight as allies of the Muslim armies. Sir Thomas Arnold, an early twentieth century orientalist, gives an example of a Christian Arab tribe that avoided paying the *jizya* altogether by fighting alongside Muslim armies: *"such was the case with the tribe of al-Jurajimah, a Christian tribe in the neighborhood of Antioch, who made peace with the Muslims, promising to be their allies and fight on their side in battle, on condition that they should not be called upon to pay jizya and should receive their proper share of the booty."*

So this verse came after many treaties were made with non-Muslim populations who did not want to fight with the Muslim armies. Because of this, they are required to pay the *jizya* tax. If they refuse this, only then does the command to fight apply.

More importantly to our discussion, this particular verse was revealed directly in response to the Jews in Khaybar, *not* the Christians or the Zoroastrians at all. Even then, it was not all Jewish tribes; it was only the tribes of Khaybar who started plotting with the Byzantine Empire, even though they had agreed to be vassals to the Prophet. And that was why the Prophet led his Companions on several campaigns against them before and after the conquest of Mecca.

I hope this answers your questions, Roger, and I look forward to your response.

May peace be with you,
Ahmed

Email #06 – From: Roger
Sent: Tuesday, September 15, 2015 2:14 p.m.

Ahmed,

Hope your mom is okay. No rush. I do appreciate your time.

I understand the point on taxes. However, almost all of the translations define the taxes levied on Christians and others for the following reasons: subjugation (Yusaf Ali, Shakir), humbled (Sahih Int), and brought low (Khan). I am not sure those would be the words for taxes given for protection so much as in fear.

I just don't see Sura 9:29, 9:30, 9.31 being specifically about taxes; it is about the belief that Jesus is the messiah to Christians. There are also Suras 5.72 and 5.63. Which brings me to my question: If someone believes that Jesus is the messiah and does not believe Muhammad is a prophet, does that qualify as an unbeliever?

If someone is an unbeliever, are they not subject to punishment under Muslim scripture (9:123), (3:28), and (66:9), etc.?

With regard to friendships with unbelievers, the Qur'an says in Sura 5:50-51, 3:28, 3:118-119, etc., not to be friends with unbelievers. I cannot really see the only reason for this scripture

5:51 being to just get Muslims to band together for protection; he calls in 5:51 Christian evildoers, unjust, wrongdoers (various translations).

As for my question before, I did not get a clear response: Can the claim that Islam is a peaceful religion be made if there are clearly non-peaceful texts?

Email #07 – From: Ahmed Rashed
Sent: Saturday, September 19, 2015 8:40 a.m.

In the Name of God; Most Gracious, Most Merciful:

Good afternoon, Roger:

Let us start with your last question first: Can Islam be called a religion of peace if it has non-peaceful verses? Yes, it can. Being a peaceful religion does not mean being a pacifist religion. A peaceful religion can justify the use of force if the goal of that force is maintaining peace, justice, and law. Islam teaches that it is permissible to use force to check aggression, protect the weak from the depredations of the strong, and apply capital punishment against those who are convicted of capital crimes. A pacifist religion would see a police force, an army, and laws permitting self-defense as immoral. However, a peaceful religion would see those as moral and necessary instruments to promote the common peace. Muslims are commanded to seek peace, but we are free to defend ourselves if attacked. And yes, we agree that extremists have taken this totally to the extreme. That is why moderate Muslims like me and many organizations like WhyIslam.org have been speaking out against them.

As for friendships with unbelievers, every single verse in the Qur'an on this topic uses the term *"awliya,"* which as I mentioned in the previous email means "patron" or "ally." The Arabic term for "friends" is *"sahaba."* I stand by my previous statement, as all the Qur'an scholars agree that the verses you cited were revealed in the context of intertribal conflict and the issue of whether it is permissible for the Muslim community to ally with non-Muslims in the defense of their homes and lives. As

I mentioned in the previous email, if friendships in the general sense were scripturally prohibited, how could the Qur'an allow marriage between Muslim men and Jewish or Christian women? Moderate Muslims all over the world understand these verses in this way. The opinions of violent Muslims do not concern us because they are not the mainstream interpretation.

As for verses (9:123), (3:28), and (66:9), these are all talking about the non-Muslims who were fighting the Prophet and already at war with them. The context of revelation clearly shows this. The general rule for how Muslims are expected to behave with non-Muslims is this:

God does not forbid you to deal kindly and justly with anyone who has not fought you for your faith or driven you out of your homes: God loves the just. But God forbids you to take as allies those who have fought against you for your faith, driven you out of your homes, and helped others to drive you out: any of you who take them as allies will truly be wrongdoers. (60:8-9)

So God REQUIRES that Muslims treat peaceful non-Muslims with goodness and equality.

Regarding *jizya*, the submission mentioned in the verse refers to submission to political authority and humility due to their agreement to be vassals of the Prophet and the Muslim polity in Medina. Remember the history of these revelations: people had already entered into a pact with the Prophet (pbuh). It was common at the time of revelation that a community would pay tribute to another community as a sign that they had no hostile intents and that they accepted the latter community as authority. These verses were revealed in that historical reality, and since the Prophet lived in that reality, the Qur'an revealed instructions that were culturally appropriate. Whenever the Prophet had to mobilize his community to fight aggression, he and the early Muslims would fight until the enemy tribe was defeated or surrendered. The terms of surrender usually included tribute, a payment as a sign that the former aggressors would not cause trouble.

This is exactly what happened to the Jewish tribe in Khaybar. The command to fight them was not triggered by their refusal to enter Islam; the Qur'an clearly states, **"There is no compulsion in faith."** Rather, the command was triggered by their political ambitions to undermine and attack the nascent Muslim community. The overwhelming majority of moderate Muslims classify the *dhimma* system, and therefore *jizya*, as ahistorical in the sense that it is inappropriate for the age of nation-states and democracies. Therefore, we see these verses in their context, understand their wisdom at the time of revelation, and also understand that they are no longer relevant today.

May peace be with you,
Ahmed

Email #02 – From: Roger
Sent: Monday, September 21, 2015 3:15 p.m.

Ahmed,

Whether in the context of war or otherwise, I see no peaceful recourse for the Suras 5.63-5.95. Muhammad is saying here that Christians and Jews are wrong for their belief that Jesus is the messiah (in the case of Christians) and that they will be punished. Now, the fact that Jews and Muslims fought one another can somewhat justify the violent suras against them, but again Christians, as you said, fought with Muhammad, and in the case of the Ethiopians saved many of them from death. Sura 5.69 clearly states that belief in Muhammad as a prophet is part of being a believer.

Sura 5.73 is directed at Christians as Muhammad's revelations, says that God will **"afflict the disbelievers among them a painful punishment."**

Sura 5.86 goes on to say, **"but those who disbelieved and denied our signs are the companion of Hellfire."**

Ahmed, whether this is metaphorical or not is irrelevant, because unfortunately these suras are clearly exacting non-peaceful judgement on Christians, and others against those who do not believe. It is very confusing, as our first email started to figure out what peaceful and non-peaceful texts abrogate one another, or if they in fact abrogate one another. Unfortunately, I feel it is too easy to extrapolate and justify violence against other religions just because of their perceived "unbelief."

I do appreciate you taking the time. I really hope that your interpretation wins out across the Muslim world and becomes the loud majority. I believe in focusing on the strengths that bind us rather than what divides us. Part of my questioning was dealing with inconsistencies with the peaceful parts of the Qur'an when I read it years ago.

As a fellow believer in Christ's holiness, I will leave you with this quote from C.S. Lewis:

"I am trying here to prevent anyone saying the really foolish thing that people often say about Him: I'm ready to accept Jesus as a great moral teacher, but I don't accept his claim to be God. That is the one thing we must not say. A man who was merely a man and said the sort of things Jesus said would not be a great moral teacher. He would either be a lunatic — on the level with the man who says he is a poached egg — or else he would be the Devil of Hell. You must make your choice. Either this man was, and is, the Son of God, or else a madman or something worse. You can shut him up for a fool, you can spit at him and kill him as a demon or you can fall at his feet and call him Lord and God, but let us not come with any patronizing nonsense about his being a great human teacher. He has not left that open to us. He did not intend to."

Thanks again, guys,
May God's peace and love be on you all,
Roger

Email #09 – From: Ahmed Rashed
Sent: Monday, September 21, 2015 4:29 p.m.

In the Name of God; Most Gracious, Most Merciful:

Good afternoon, Roger:

I pray this email finds you in the best of health and faith,

God willing. I am saddened that you ended your message with a farewell, as if you intended to close this conversation, and with it the doors of dialogue.

How is there no peaceful recourse? Verses 5:63–5:95 are only a theological refutation of the concept of Jesus's divinity. It is not a call to physically attack Christians. There is no punishment for calling Jesus (pbuh) the Messiah; in fact, Muslims also call him *Al-Massih,* which means the "Anointed One," which is the same meaning as the Greek *Christos* (Christ). The "punishment" described here is in the hereafter, not in this worldly life, and it is for ascribing divinity to Jesus. Yes, this is obviously a clear theological difference between the two faiths, but it is NOT a call to violence. It is NOT a statement against peaceful coexistence.

On the contrary, we read this:

Those who believe, and the Jews, and the Sabians, and the Christians — whoever believes in God and the Last Day, and does what is right — they have nothing to fear, nor shall they grieve. (5:69)

So those who are Jews and Christians who believe in God's Oneness and the Last day and do good works, they shall be rewarded.

I think the verses that make you feel that there can be no peace are 5:72-74 which specifically call out and disclaim the belief that Jesus was God or the son of God. It finishes the argument with this:

Say, "O People of the Scripture! Do not exaggerate in your religion beyond the truth; and do not follow the opinions of people who went astray before, and misled many, and themselves strayed off the balanced way." (5:77)

But this is *not* a call to attack or do violence to someone who believes this. Rather, it is a sincere advice and admonition that ascribing divinity to anything other than God is misguidance. The language is strong because the spirit behind the advice is compassion and caring for the well-being and final destination of the listener. Nowhere in these passages is there a teaching that Christians should be fought, persecuted, or ridiculed.

Instead we read this:

[O Prophet,] You will find that the people most hostile towards the believers are the Jews and the polytheists. And you will find that the nearest in affection towards the believers are those who say, "We are Christians." That is because among them are priests and monks, and they are not arrogant. (5:82)

So this is actually saying the opposite of what you claim.
Remember, with dialogue comes understanding.
May peace be with you,
Ahmed

Email #10 – From: Roger
Sent: Saturday, September 26, 2015 3:26 p.m.

Not closing the dialogue, fellas; I just think we are at an impasse of sorts. I hear all that you are saying, but each time I read the Qur'an, I think to myself that what you're saying is a stretch. It's as if what I am reading does not mean what it says according to our dialogue. I hope and pray that your interpretations are correct and become common Islamic theological thinking.

Trust me, brothers, you all will be the first folks I reach out to when I have more questions. You have been gracious with your time, and I really do appreciate it.

Email #11 – From: Ahmed Rashed
Sent: Monday, September 28, 2015 11:02 a.m.

In the Name of God; Most Gracious, Most Merciful:

Good morning, Roger:

I understand your sentiment. There is an ideological battle going on now within the Muslim world for the "Soul of Islam." On the one hand there are the extremists who see everything in polarizing black and white, and then there are the moderates who consider the context and nuances of the scriptures. You can read more about the moderate Muslim view (and their refutation of extremists) in Omid Safi's book, *Progressive Muslims: On Justice, Gender, and Pluralism*.

I also hope the moderate and nuanced view wins out, and for that reason, we here at WhyIslam.org are committed to speaking out against the extreme interpretations in our faith tradition and setting the record straight to the best of our abilities. I am glad that you see us as a resource for understanding, and I look forward to any other questions or discussion topics you would like to bring to the table.

May peace be with you,
Ahmed

With Dialogue Comes Understanding

CONVERSATION WITH NEIL

The Remembrance of God

Email #02 – From: Neil
Sent: Wednesday, September 16, 2015 3:52 p.m.

Mr. Rashed,
Thank you for the introduction. I do have a few questions. What is meant exactly by "remembrance of God?" I hear that term a lot and am not sure what is meant by that exactly. Why would an omnipotent being have a need or care whether we remember him or not?

Also, Muslims believe that there were thousands of prophets, so does Islam have a means of determining who was a prophet and who is just proclaiming himself a prophet? Were women ever considered prophets? Exactly which prophets from the Bible does Islam believe and which does Islam reject? Does a prophet self-identify as a prophet?

Finally, why is belief in angels so critical?
Thank you in advance,
Neil

Email #03 – From: Ahmed Rashed
Sent: Tuesday, September 22, 2015 11:35 a.m.

In the Name of Allah; Most Gracious, Most Merciful:
Good morning, Neil:
Remembering God means developing the quality of *"taqwa;"* this is Arabic for "God-consciousness." It means living with the active realization and awareness that God is witness of all we do and that we will be accountable for those actions. It is not about God needing to be remembered; he is the Self-Sufficient. All creation is in need of Him, but He is in need of nothing. So this idea of developing God-consciousness and remembrance is that the purpose of this worldly life is the purification of the soul before it is recalled to God's presence in the after-life. Also, as mentioned in my initial email, it is by living in this mode of awareness that the human heart will find peace and tranquility. Therefore, the "remembrance of God" is both a goal that humans

should strive for to be successful in the hereafter AND a remedy that humans should use when the worldly life overwhelms them with its worries.

There are twenty-five prophets mentioned by name in the Qur'an, but the Prophet (pbuh) said that over 120,000 prophets were sent to humanity since Adam descended to Earth. There are no criteria for judging historical figures. The Qur'an is the only arbiter of who were definitely prophets or messengers. The Qur'an and the Prophet (pbuh) both say that Muhammad was the last messenger, and no more revelation would come after him, so this means that anyone who claims prophethood or receiving revelation from God after him (632 CE) is automatically declared to be false.

As for biblical figures and ancient religious leaders from other faith traditions, Islamic scholars have speculated and put forward theories, but in the end they conclude "God knows" and do not try to enforce their views. This is because such speculation is considered academic and not relevant to how people are expected to believe and behave. The Final Book and the Final Messenger have come, and they supersede all previous teachings and revelations. Both the words of the Qur'an and the teachings of the Prophet Muhammad (pbuh) are preserved and intact, so there is no doubt about what these canonical sources say.

Regarding identification, prophethood is bestowed on a person; nobody can seek it or hope to achieve it by his own actions. All prophets mentioned in the Qur'an were commissioned by God by either the Angel of Revelation (Gabriel), by prophetic dreams, or by direct speaking to God (like Moses).

There were no women prophets, and that is because prophets are expected to be rejected, ridiculed, persecuted, and maybe even tortured or abused for their preaching. Out of God's mercy, and to maintain the honor and integrity of prophethood, this difficult burden has only been commissioned to men.

As for why belief in angels is one of the core articles of Islamic faith, angels are an important part of God's creation, for God uses them to act as messengers between Himself and mankind. The Angel Gabriel is the Angel of Revelation; he is responsible for delivering the revelation of God to all the prophets in general, and to the Prophet Muhammad in particular. The Angel of Death takes the souls of all those who die. There are also two angels assigned to every person; one recording the good deeds and the other recording the bad deeds. So much of the understanding of God's relationship with humanity hinges on the role of angels; therefore, believing in them is required to have correct faith in God and the mechanics of salvation.

Let me know if you have any other questions or would like to discuss these topics in more detail.

May peace be with you,
Ahmed

Email #04 – From: Neil
Sent: Sunday, September 27, 2015 5:56 p.m.

Thank you for answering that. I actually do not think that *taqwa*, as you say, is really that far from what Christians believe on that issue as you describe it. That is interesting.

I would like to know more about the Qu'ran. Do you have a good way to read the Qu'ran for beginners? I have an English translation, but I have to admit I am having trouble following it. Do you have any suggestions on a study guide for newcomers? I do have a background in theology, so I can read theological texts.

Neil

Email #05 – From: Ahmed Rashed
Sent: Monday, October 5, 2015 9:42 a.m.

In the Name of Allah; Most Gracious, Most Merciful:

Good morning, Neil:

Please forgive me for taking so long to reply. I had the flu last week and could not attend to my messages.

To get to your points, it is not surprising to me that the concept of being God-fearing or God-conscience is similar in both

Christianity and Islam. After all, our Prophet Muhammad (pbuh) taught that all prophets are brothers with the same master and the same message. So we honor Jesus (pbuh) and believe that most of the teachings attributed to him came from God. The only theological difference between Islam and Christianity is the divinity of Christ (pbuh).

As for reading the Qur'an, I am curious which translation you are using? Most of my students find the Qur'an very conversational, and while some of the flow is difficult for a first-time reader, most of my students can follow without problems.

Also, if reading the Qur'an from front-to-back is confusing, it might be helpful to start with Sura (chapter) 29. Most of the suras before this one were revealed in Medina, so there is social and political context you need to be aware of to understand these chapters fully. Another option is to use the attached study guide. This is what I give to second-year students after they cover the basics of Islam. It is a series of selections picked out from the Qur'an, so you can read a selection and get back to me with reflections or questions.

Finally, if you are willing to spend some money on more rigorous study guides, these two are my recommendations:

http://www.islamicbookstore.com/b5085.html
http://www.islamicbookstore.com/b6506.html
May peace be with you,
Ahmed

Email #06 – From: Neil
Sent: Wednesday, October 7, 2015 9:27 p.m.

Ahmed,

Sorry to hear you had the flu. That is never fun. Hope you are better now.

Thank you. I will look at that outline. It was not so much that I do not understand the content, it is just, as you say, very conversational in style. I guess I am not used to that. I will look at those guides, and I am sure that will be helpful.

I would be interested in learning more about some the basic theology of Islam, particularly prayer and moral theology. Do you have any suggestions? Some of the terminology I find confusing.

Thanks,
Neil

Email #07 – From: Ahmed Rashed
Sent: Friday, October 9, 2015 11:01 a.m.

In the Name of Allah; Most Gracious, Most Merciful:

Good morning, Neil:

I am feeling better now, thank you for asking. It was just a residual cough that the doctor says will have to work itself out by itself.

As for the basic theology of Islam, you can download my Islam101 class notes and slideshows. Just go to my website (www.WhatWouldAMuslimSay.net) and subscribe. You will get the notes and slideshows delivered to your email. Listen to the slideshow, read through the notes, and then reply with questions, and we can move forward from there.

May peace be with you,
Ahmed

Conversation with Mark

The Shroud of Turin Debate

Email #02 – From: Mark
Sent: Tuesday, November 1, 2016 6:16 p.m.

Do you think the shroud provides proof of Christ's crucifixion and resurrection?
http://www.4shared.com/web/preview/pdf/qAV-W_Wrce
https://www.youtube.com/watch?v=8YbSaPRuU0M
Shukran,
Mark

Email #03 – From: Ahmed Rashed
Sent: Friday, November 4, 2016 12:26 p.m.

In the Name of God, Most Gracious, Most Compassionate:
Before we talk about the shroud, let us take a look at what the Qur'an actually says about the crucifixion:

And for their faithlessness, and their saying against Mary a monstrous slander. And for their saying, "We have killed the Messiah, Jesus, the son of Mary, the Messenger of God." In fact, they did not kill him, nor did they crucify him, but it appeared to them as if they did. Indeed, those who differ about him are in doubt about it. They have no knowledge of it, except the following of assumptions. Certainly, they did not kill him. Rather, God raised him up to Himself. God is Mighty and Wise. There is none from the People of the Scripture but will believe in him before his death, and on the Day of Resurrection he will be a witness against them. (4:156-159)

So Muslims believe he was raised up to God, not crucified. The sequence of events is not refuted; rather, the identity of the man on the cross is refuted. Therefore, we see that the information presented in the video about the shroud is not relevant to the Muslim's belief. As I said above, the Qur'an does not deny that the crucifixion itself took place; the Qur'an argues that the person who WAS crucified was not Jesus.

May peace be with you,
Ahmed

Email #04 – From: Mark
Sent: Friday, November 4, 2016 4:50 p.m.

Dear Ahmed,

Shukran for writing back to me; I am truly honored to hear from you!

I am very glad you are willing to discuss the Shroud of Turin as evidence of Jesus's death.

But despite my pleasure hearing from you, I believe that what you write here makes no sense. The Qur'an passage you cite does not deny that Jesus was crucified. Rather it seems to claim exactly what the bible claims: that death could not hold Him because God raised Him from the dead!

There is none from the People of the Scripture but will believe in him before his death, and on the Day of Resurrection he will be a witness against them. (4:156-159)

The last verse also makes no sense, for there are MANY Jews today (and all through history) who believed in Isa al Masich!

Also your claim that God would substitute an innocent victim in place of Jesus makes God an unjust monster and not worthy of praise. Jesus did not want to be saved from His enemies. He knew his entire life that he would be killed by them. And he willingly offered his life, and he forgave those who took it from him.

Finally, if you will please forgive me for perhaps overburdening you (I know software designers work very hard and long hours), please comment on the teaching of this Indian Muslim convert to Christianity:

https://www.youtube.com/watch?v=WjUXd4qW9mg
One of the most powerful testimonies I have EVER seen!!! An Indian Muslim who converted to Catholicism.
http://jerusalemchannel.tv/koran-converted-christianity/
God's Richest Blessings to You in *YaHuWAllaH*,
Mark

Email #05 – From: Mark
Sent: Friday, November 4, 2016 8:40 p.m.

Ahmed,

I have another thought to share with you.

I think the Qur'anic passage you sent to me is ambiguous and might mean that Jesus really was crucified, but death couldn't hold Him because God raised Him up.

But if you could prove to me that the Qur'an means what most Muslims say, namely that God raised Jesus to Heaven before He died and substituted someone else on the cross for Him, then I would say the following:

As you probably know, the four Gospels present different stories about Jesus's life. The one thing they ALL agree on, however, is that Jesus died on the cross and was raised from the dead three days later. This is ironclad agreement between all the Gospels, as well as the letters that make up the rest of the New Testament.

Even the many different Christian churches and denominations ALL agree that Jesus died on the cross and was raised from the dead. Catholics, Greek Orthodox, Protestants, Anglicans, Baptists, Seventh-day Adventists, Jehovah's Witnesses, Pentecostals, Charismatics, and Mormons ALL agree that Jesus died and was resurrected.

Indeed, the Apostle Paul writes that this is the very HEART of the Christian religion. So be clear that on Christ's death and resurrection no Christian can compromise. So what do we do with the Qur'anic claim that (perhaps) another was substituted for Jesus on the cross?

With all due respect to you, Ahmed, and I do respect Islam deeply, we cannot accept this claim of the Qur'an. Look at it from our perspective. We have Christian texts and fundamental beliefs for six hundred years before Muhammad revealed the Qur'an. These beliefs are unanimous about Jesus's death and resurrection. The burden of proof, then, if you want to undo or deconstruct these central cherished Christian beliefs, is on YOU and all

Muslims to demonstrate that Jesus did not die on the cross. You cannot hope to persuade us simply by referring to the Sura in question. We will not accept that interpretation of it. It's that simple.

Even secular historians say that Jesus's crucifixion and resurrection are among the best verified events in history. A few verses from your Qur'an cannot possibly undo that reality.

I hope you will forgive me for speaking so firmly and disrespectfully about your holy book. There is much that is beautiful in your religion. But we cannot accept or respect your efforts to rewrite our own Christian beliefs and realities. You are the newcomers on the scene, and if you want to rewrite our religious history, you will have to bring convincing proofs.

If you have any thoughts to share I would be happy to read them, Inshallah. God Bless You, Ahmed, and thank you for allowing me to express these thoughts to you,

In Christ, *Yessua al Masich*,
Mark

Email #06 – From: Ahmed Rashed
Sent: Monday, November 7, 2016 10:28 a.m.

In the Name of God; Most Gracious, Most Merciful:

Good morning, Mark:

Let us step back for a moment. This is an academic discussion, not a confessional one. The purpose was not to convince you but rather to clearly explain the philosophy and understanding that Muslim scholars have had and continue to have on the subject. The goal of WhyIslam.org is to provide accurate information about the mainstream interpretation of Islam, not to prove its credentials or truth claims.

Regarding the Muslim view of crucifixion, our teachers teach what is written in the Qur'an: that it appeared to the enemies of Christ that he was crucified. The verse is clear and unambiguous: **In fact, they did not kill him, nor did they crucify him, but it appeared to them as if they did.**

Therefore, the Christian view of the crucifixion does in fact contradict Islamic teachings, just as the Islamic teachings on the crucifixion do in fact contradict Christian teachings. These are irreconcilable theologies, and this is something that mature scholars of both traditions have admitted and agreed upon since the beginning.

The question, "What to do" about one scripture or another is for each seeker to come to their own conclusions about. A seeker who finds the truth claim of the Bible stronger will accept that view and accept Christianity. On the other hand, a seeker who finds the truth claim of the Qur'an stronger will accept that view and accept Islam. While we realize that both cannot be simultaneously true, we leave it to the seeker to decide which path he or she ultimately chooses to follow.

May peace be with you,
Ahmed

Email #07 – From: Mark
Sent: Monday, November 7, 2016 2:32 p.m.

Ahmed,

Thanks for writing back!

You left off this important part of the Sura that makes it totally conform to the Christian teaching.

Anyway, as I said before, if the Qur'an really does teach that Jesus was not crucified, in contradiction to all Christian writings and history, then the onus is on Muslims to demonstrate why anyone should believe this to be true.

And you have not done that.

How can you decide a truth claim of something that contradicts history?

For example, if someone produced a book that claimed Christopher Columbus never sailed across the Atlantic, how would one assess that?

Would one pray to know if it was true, or would one consult historical evidence?

So it seems Muslims must do about Christ's resurrection.
May peace be with you too,
Mark

Email #08 – From: Ahmed Rashed
Sent: Tuesday, November 8, 2016 12:17 p.m.

In the Name of God; Most Gracious, Most Merciful:

Good morning, Mark:

First of all, I did not leave off the most important part of the Sura. This sentence was included in my original email to you about why Muslims do not believe that Christ himself was crucified. If you remember, you claimed that the passage in the Qur'an was "ambiguous," so I was responding to your claim by pointing out that exact sentence that clearly states that Jesus (pbuh) was not killed nor crucified. REMEMBER, our purpose is only to present accurate information about the teachings of Islam. You questioned whether the Qur'an actually contests Jesus's crucifixion, and I replied to assure you that "yes," the Qur'an and all the scholars in Islam's history have been reading their scripture correctly.

Secondly, this snippet of the Qur'an does not confirm the teachings of Christianity because the verse just before it asserts that Jesus (pbuh) was not killed nor crucified. The whole point of Christianity is that Jesus died and was then resurrected and was then raised up to God. The whole point of the Islam is that Jesus was raised up to God without dying or resurrecting. Therefore, the verses in the Qur'an are very much against the teachings of Christianity.

Third, there is no onus on Muslims whatsoever. You may believe what you want to believe, and I may believe what I want to believe. There is no contradiction with history because the Qur'an does not deny that SOMEONE died on the cross. The Qur'an only denies that the person who died on the cross was Jesus (pbuh). This is within the historical records. Someone died on the cross. Christianity and Islam and history agree on this point. That someone looked like Jesus. Christianity and Islam and history agree on this point. That someone was then interred. Christianity and Islam and history agree on this point. That dead person disappeared a few days later. Christianity and Islam and history agree on this point.

However, Islam *disagrees* with Christianity on who that person really was. Islam disagrees with Christianity on why that person disappeared. History *is silent* on these two questions and has no facts or evidence to present either way. We know how some of the people of that time interpreted these events, but the Christian community did not come to a consensus on which interpretation to adopt until the Council of Nicea over three hundred years after the events took place. This is historical fact. The identity of the person crucified is not independently verifiable, and the Qur'an offers an alternative sequence of events that fits the historical evidence.

Therefore, it is perfectly reasonable and within a person's right, whether they are Muslim or not, to reject the Christian interpretation of crucifixion. There are many people in this world who do not accept Jesus as their savior. Most of those people are not Muslims, my friend; they are Hindu, Buddhist, or agnostic, atheist, or otherwise. If the details of the crucifixion were so historically clear and irreducible, then every person would have no choice but to accept Jesus in this way, as you have been saying. However, the details are not so historically clear or irreducible, so accepting Jesus is still a matter of faith, not a matter of fact.

Incidentally, this is true of any religion, even Islam. Yes, I have my rational reasons why I believe Islam to be the "Truth," but even these reasons are tempered by a personal faith. It is that personal faith that makes each person's religion his or her own. We can present all the "proofs" in the world, but at the end of the day, there will always be room for doubt. This is how God wills it. Faith springs from the depths of the heart and then accepted by the mind; not the other way around.

May peace be with you,
Ahmed

Email #09 – From: Mark
Sent: Thursday, November 10, 2016 7:55 p.m.

Salaam Aleikum Ahmed,

I have been thinking more about your claim that Jesus never was crucified but rather was raptured to Heaven while another was falsely substituted for Him on the cross.

The more I think about this, the more angry I become. Your claim is absurd on so many different levels, it's hard to know where to begin. You claim Islam honors Jesus as the Jewish Messiah. Yet you deny the heart of His mission as reported to us by the New Testament. It also invalidates our entire religion, which is based on the atoning power of Jesus's death on the cross, followed by His glorious Resurrection!

This is no simple matter, Ahmed. Islam has essentially tampered with our Scriptures, and G+D promises severe punishments to anyone who alters His Holy Word!

I always have admired Islam, at least since the time when I got to know the Muslim doctors in an Israeli hospital where I was treated back in the 1990s. I spent a lot of time talking with the male Palestinian nurses and learned a lot about Islam, and I was amazed at how similar it is to Judaism. I also came to admire Islamic culture, with its emphasis on modesty in dress and behavior, cleanliness, and hygiene, and submission to our Creator.

Since returning to the land of my birth, America, in 2006, I have been dismayed to see the hostility of American Christians to Islam and their almost automatic favoritism to and sympathy for Judaism. This never made sense to me, and I fought it hard. I even introduced my Hebrew-Arabic name for God, YAHUWALLAH, as a way to combat this prejudice.

I also long have pondered which is worse: Judaism's open hostility to Jesus or Islam's twisted admiration for Him. It seemed to me that both were equally bad distortions of the Truth.

But now that you have dialogued with me and explained so clearly Islam's position nullifying the crucifixion of Christ, I am leaning to the view that in God's eyes, Islam is WORSE than Judaism; MUCH WORSE. That's because of the principle that it is easier to deal with an overt enemy than with a false friend.

Now I am perceiving, thanks mainly to our correspondence, that the open hostility of Judaism to Christianity is much less dangerous than the false and distorted friendship of Islam. The Islamic Jesus is so different from the Christian Jesus that we are talking about two completely different persons. The Islamic Jesus also is a false prophet for Christians, since He prophesied His death and resurrection and then avoided them. Judaism doesn't reform Jesus but denies Him exactly as portrayed by the New Testament. Judaism doesn't try to substitute a recreated Jesus in place of the Christian one.

I am thankful to you for helping me to recognize this. However, I also am very saddened because my spirit senses the grave peril you and all Muslims are in for denying the Truth about Jesus Christ of Nazareth. The sin of the Muslim apologists (like you) and imams and sheiks and other religious teachers and leaders is much greater than the sin of the average Muslim who doesn't understand these matters. I truly shudder for you, Ahmed.

I have long been a 9/11 Truther, believing that the attacks were falsely blamed on Muslims as a way to promote the New World Order. But now I am wondering if G+D allowed such deception because Islam itself is at heart an enormous deception!

You also should be aware that prominent Israelis who have the ear of the American military are proposing destroying the Kaaba at Mecca as a way to subdue Islamic terrorism. Netanyahu is now claiming that Hitler himself never designed to exterminate the Jews but was prevailed to do so by the Mufti of Jerusalem, who was allied with Germany in WWII. Clearly, global wrath is building against Islam.

Jesus caused the beautiful Jerusalem temple to be destroyed due to the false worship and abuses of the Jewish religious leadership. Certainly He can do the same to the heart of Islam in Mecca if your religion also is promoting false teachings and distortions of the true Messianic Hope of the world!

Please ponder and pray about what I have written.

I realize that for you to accept the fullness of Truth about Jesus Christ might entail a lot of personal sacrifice and suffering. Perhaps ostracism from your family and country. Perhaps worse. But I would encourage you, at the very least, to desist from serving as an Islamic apologist until the truth of this matter is resolved in your heart, because you would not want to serve as a stumbling block to the weak and innocent members of the House of Islam!

I am praying for you, my friend.

InShallah my friend Ahmed you too will be counted among the Saints of the Almighty YAHUWALLAH.

Amen.

Mark

Email #10 – From: Ahmed Rashed
Sent: Fri, Nov 11, 2016 9:09 a.m.

In the Name of God, Most Gracious, Most Merciful:

My dear Mark, what is the purpose of this email? Really, are we trying to come to understanding or are we trying to descend into argumentative polemics?

Your anger is misplaced, Mark. Unitarian Christians have similar views about Jesus as Muslims; do they make you angry? How about Jehovah's Witnesses or United Pentecostal Church International or the Unity School of Christianity? I have worked in interfaith dialogue for over fifteen years now, and your view of Christ is not the only one, even among those who call themselves Christians.

May peace be with you,

Ahmed

Email #11 – From: Mark
Sent: Friday, November 11, 2016 2:56 p.m.

All of these groups agree that Jesus died on the cross and was resurrected after three days in the tomb. Stop obfuscating and lying! I cannot continue to dialogue with you, Ahmed.

I told you there is much in Islam I respect. But you have dangerously distorted the truth about the God-Man Jesus. And now I place you at the foot of the cross for God to instruct you directly.

Shalom wa Salaam.

Email #12 – From: Mark
Sent: Friday, November 11, 2016 6:16 p.m.

Dear Ahmed,

A friend named Robert asked me to forward to you his attached peace plan for the Middle East. It is based on spiritual values. Robert is a Jewish believer in Jesus with great esteem for Islam. I would be happy if the three of us could communicate our thoughts about this.

Also please forgive me for writing to you with anger and impatience.

Shalom wa Salaam,
Mark

Email #13 – From: Ahmed Rashed
Sent: Wednesday, November 16, 2016 12:45 p.m.

In the Name of God, Most Gracious, Most Compassionate:

Dear Mark,

Thank you for sharing this with me. I will start reading it today, God willing. Then we can all share our thoughts about it.

May peace be with you,
Ahmed

Conversation with Trevon

Why Is There Conflict in the Middle East?

Email #02 – From: Trevon
Sent: Monday, August 29, 2016 3:50 p.m.

I've been wondering about something. I was raised Christian. I'm not anything at the moment, but I've been studying Islam because of my friend Jason. I found this quote in the Qur'an that had me puzzled. It's Qur'an 2:62. Does it mean that even if Christians and Jews don't believe in the Qur'an, do they still get into Heaven or Paradise? Jews and Christians believe in different things than what Islam teaches, and I don't get how they would get into Paradise if they didn't believe in the Qur'an and worship Allah. Another thing about Qur'an 2:62 that has me confused is if Christians and Jews are not a problem, why is there such conflict over there in the Middle East?

Email #03 – From: Ahmed Rashed
Sent: Tuesday, August 30, 2016 2:48 p.m.

In the Name of God, Most Gracious, Most-Merciful:
Good morning, Trevon:

It is nice to hear from you again. Regarding the verse you mention, the traditional interpretation is that it refers to the original Christians, Jews, and Sabians who followed the authentic teachings of their prophets before the coming of Prophet Muhammad (pbuh). This verse was revealed when one of the Prophet's Companions asked about his old Christian teachers. This Companion was told by them about a prophet that was due to appear in the Arab lands, but they died before they could travel with him to Arabia.

The criteria for salvation is following the **original** message that has come to you; so those who only heard about Jesus or only about Moses would be held accountable for that prophet's *authentic* teachings. It would be injustice for God to judge people who never even heard of Jesus why they still follow Moses' book. Likewise, it would be injustice for Him to judge people who never heard of Muhammad about why they still follow Jesus.

Islam teaches that Jesus (pbuh) did not actually preach that he was divine or the concept of Trinity, so Muslims believe that those who ascribe divinity to him will be challenged by Jesus on the Day of Judgment. Ultimately, God will be just and impartial; for God never does injustice to His creatures.

As for why there is so much strife in the Middle East, the fighting is about land, resources, and self-determination, NOT RELIGION. The original conflict was between the Muslim Ottoman Empire and their subjects. Each province wanted autonomy for its own ethnic group and region. After World War I, the Ottoman Empire was carved up into British and French mandates. Then the conflict of these peoples was again for the cause of autonomy against these Western empires. Just as the last of these mandates were dismantled, the Zionist movement established the State on Israel on Palestinian land. The Zionists had the backing of the British Empire and also the support of many countries of the United Nations. This was seen by the Palestinian people (and their Arab neighbors) as unjust colonization. This was the beginning of the worst conflict and strife as people fought for their homeland. The Zionists fought for what they claimed was an existential need and their scriptural birthright. The Arabs fought for their ancestral homes and against what they could only describe as ethnic cleansing.

The conflict has been ongoing since then. With this background, the surrounding Arab nations became more and more autocratic and dictatorial, so we see the Arab Spring begin in 2011 ... which was once again a cry for self-determination and autonomy of the people, rather than elite, nepotistic Arab families. As the Arab Spring degenerated into civil wars in multiple areas, radical groups like ISIS sprang up to fill in the power vacuum of the weakened Arab governments.

While radical groups do hold religious supremacist ideologies, the main reason for all the fighting is simply people wanting self-determination and rights to benefit from their natural resources without exploitation from external powers or internal Mafia families. Until there emerges a set of governments that legitimately and faithfully represents the peoples they govern, most historians and political scientists predict that such strife will continue.

May peace be with you,
Ahmed

Email #04 – From: Trevon
Sent: Monday, September 5, 2016 3:19 p.m.

Sorry, Ahmed, for taking so long to write back to this one. I've been busy this week.

I thought all the conflict in the Middle East is about religion. You hear groups like ISIS who talk about spreading the religion by force and trying to make it a worldwide caliphate. They go destroying old religious sites and killing people who don't convert. I thought the whole goal of the group was to make it a Muslim world where we worship only one god, getting rid of false gods and getting rid of its followers. I saw in the YouTube movie, ISLAM: WHAT THE WEST NEEDS TO KNOW, that Muhammad killed six hundred Jews in one day. I've heard countless times that ISIS is just trying to get back to the early days of Islam and act how the Prophet did. When you talked about the Zionist movement establishing the state on Israel on Palestinian land, I'm not surprised. In America we have a lot of anti-Semitism and there is a lot said about how they control the media, the banks, and everything else.

Email #05 – From: Ahmed Rashed
Sent: Tuesday, September 6, 2016 10:10 a.m.

In the Name of God, Most Gracious, Most-Merciful:

Good morning, Trevon.

Yes, I know that many people (including ISIS) think all the conflict is about religion. I am giving a weary sigh as I write this, but this is one of the major misconceptions that people in the West have about Islam and Muslims. Look, my friend, if it was about religion, WHY are the majority of ISIS victims Muslims? This group operates on the border between Syria, Iraq, and Turkey. These are Muslim countries that are not currently occupied, right? So who was killed when ISIS carved out a space for itself? ISIS killed soldiers of the Iraqi, Syrian, and Turkish governments; they were Muslims. While it is true that many non-Muslim villagers were pillaged, raped, and massacred, the majority of those killed were Muslims.

So this group kills Muslim soldiers of other countries and violates Islamic law regarding non-Muslim noncombatants to boot. The Prophet Muhammad CLEARLY forbade his soldiers from attacking noncombatants. His Companions also followed his example and allowed non-Muslim subjects to continue living and following whatever religion they wished so long as they did not rebel. Iraq had many Muslim sects living in it; it also has Christians and Jews living in it. All were living side by side just fine before the American invasion of 2003. There were of course flashpoints from time to time, but overall there was civil society. All that changed with the invasion. The power structure was shattered, and every group started killing each other to vie for power and wealth in the new reality.

The Shia of Iraq received US backing, so they went from being disenfranchised to being the party in power. The Sunnis of Iraq were unfortunately not able to maintain any political presence due to their repeated boycotts of the political process the US put in place, so now they are the disenfranchised party. The Kurds of Iraq have always pushed for more autonomy, and they were savvy enough to get that from the new Shia Iraq government. So with the Sunnis marginalized and the Shia committing the same prejudices against the Sunnis that the Sunnis committed against the Shia, what you see is simply phase two of that power struggle over oil, land, prestige, and status.

As for whether ISIS and similar groups are representative of mainstream Islam and the example of the Prophet and his Companions, most reputable scholars identify ISIS as the Neo-Khawarij. See this link for what the original Khawarij did to the

Prophet's Companions: https://en.wikipedia.org/wiki/Khawarij

Judge for yourself if these people practiced Islam as the Prophet's Companions and disciples did.

Finally, that YouTube movie is biased and false. The Prophet never killed six hundred Jews in one day. This statement conflates the aftermath of the Battle of Bani Qurayza. Here is their story in brief:

The Bani Qurayza was a Jewish tribe that lived in Medina and had a pact of mutual defense with the Prophet. When the Meccan army amassed the pagans of north, south, and east Arabia to invade Medina, it was expected that Bani Qurayza would uphold their pact and keep their doors shut to these invaders. However, they betrayed their pact with the Prophet by holding secret negotiations with the Meccans to let this huge army enter the fortifications of Medina on condition that they would be spared and that they could share in the spoils. The Prophet learned of this and sent a recent convert to sow distrust between the invading factions. This stratagem worked, and the invaders abandoned Medina when a fierce windstorm struck at night. After the Meccans left, the Muslims laid siege to the Qurayza tribe and forced them to surrender. At this point, judgment was passed against their treachery.

Now, the YouTube video — based on the Biography of Ibn Ishaq — claims that at least four hundred and up to seven hundred Jewish men were executed. However, almost all contemporaries of Ibn Ishaq criticize him for putting narrations of questionable authenticity in his books. In addition, other narrations only list twenty-three to twenty-five people who were executed: those who were leaders in the tribe's treason or those who actually fought against the Muslims during the invasion. This number is more in line with the principles of Islamic justice (only the guilty should be punished) and more in line with physical evidence (there is no mass grave in Medina). It is for this reason that most Muslim scholars reject the story of six hundred Jews killed in a day.

See this link for more details, especially the seven reasons why this story is discounted:

http://www.haqq.com.au/~salam/misc/qurayza.html

May peace be with you,
Ahmed

Email #06 – From: Trevon
Sent: Friday, September 9, 2016 4:11 p.m.

I've read that most of the groups over there can justify their actions because of stuff they've read out of the Hadith. If the Qur'an is the word of God, shouldn't they be following that instead of what they read from other people's accounts of the Prophet?

With those groups judging who is a Muslim and who isn't, do the victims go to Paradise as martyrs since they died for being Muslims, even though the people who killed them say they weren't? And do the Muslims who kill them go to Hell for killing them and doing other stuff the Qur'an says isn't right? I read something in the Qur'an that was like, *"if you kill one person it's as if you killed all mankind but if you save one man it's as if you saved all mankind."* I'm not surprised that the video I watched was complete BS. I looked up one of the guys from the video, and it said that story he told couldn't be proven and how people think he's a liar in the east.

Email #07 – From: Ahmed Rashed
Sent: Tuesday, September 13, 2016 12:18 p.m.

In the Name of God, Most Gracious, Most-Merciful:

Good morning, Trevon.

So this is a complicated subject. The sayings of the Prophet (pbuh) explain and expound the verses of the Qur'an. Mainstream scholars teach us that both are required for proper understanding of Islam. The Qur'an and the sayings are complementary canonical sources of religious faith and practice.

Having said that, realize that most of the sayings that extremists use to justify their actions are in fact authentic. "Authentic" means that Muslim scholars have studied both the content and the chain-of-narrations of the Saying and concluded that it can be traced back to the Prophet with some confidence. The problem with extremists is when they take sayings that were made in a particular historical circumstance and apply it in a general way. So, for example, just before a major battle, the Prophet (pbuh) would exhort his troops to fight hard and kill as many of the enemy as they could. This is understood by mainstream scholars as a simple "pep-talk" to the soldiers before facing an enemy that has already driven them from their homes, stolen their properties, tortured their kinsmen, and made overtures of peace that were then treacherously betrayed. **That** is the context. An extremist group will take this saying and teach its followers that this is the general rule of how Muslims are supposed to treat non-Muslims or "bad" Muslims.

Not only do they misrepresent these sayings, but they also ignore OTHER sayings that show how the Prophet (pbuh) was tolerant and merciful to other people in general cases.

Finally, regarding the victims of these killings, there are several sayings of the Prophet (pbuh) defining who is considered a martyr (*shaheed*) in Islam:

"*There are five kinds of martyrs: One who dies of plague; one who dies of a disease of the stomach or intestines; one who drowns; one who is crushed in a collapsing building; and one who is killed in the way of God.*" [Al-Bukhari, Muslim, Malik]

"*He who is killed in the way of God is a martyr; he who dies of plague is a martyr; a woman who dies due to pregnancy and a woman who dies during delivery, her baby will pull her into Paradise with the umbilical cord.*" [Musnad Ahmad]

"*The one who dies of Dhaatul-Janb is a martyr.*" [Ibn Hibban]
NOTE: *Dhatul-Janb* is a disease in which a swelling happens under the ribs that could lead to death. Contemporary Muslim scholars use this narration to conclude that those who die from cancer are covered under the same category.

"He who dies defending his property is a martyr; he who dies in defense of his own life is a martyr; he who dies in defense of his faith is a martyr; and he who dies in defense of his family is a martyr." Al-Tabarani.

"Dying in fire is a martyrdom." Al-Tabarani and Ibn Hibban.

The phrase "*killed in the way of God*" means those Muslims who were killed while defending their faith. As for those who kill unjustly, the Qur'an does in fact say that the killer will go to Hell for that act. Being Muslim does not change the punishment of a sin. Also, the victim being Muslim or non-Muslim does not change the punishment of this sin. Islamic law allows lethal force only in the following three specific cases related to establishing justice:

a) Governments executing individuals convicted of murder or treason or any other capital crime.

b) Individuals killing life-threatening aggressors in self-defense or in defense of their home or loved-ones.

c) Soldiers killing other soldiers ON THE BATTLEFIELD.

Any killing other than these is unlawful. There are many verses in the Qur'an and many sayings of the Prophet (pbuh) that explicitly state that those who kill another soul outside of these conditions will be in Hellfire.

May peace be with you,
Ahmed

With Dialogue Comes Understanding

Conversation with Chris

A Muslim–Christian Dialogue

Email #02 – From: Chris
Sent: Thursday, December 3, 2015 8:40 p.m.

Hello! Since you have invited me to dialogue, I do have a few questions to ask.

I would first like to ask about the corruption of the faith. It has been said that Judaism and Christianity (and probably all religion in the end) was once Islam, which is the state of being in sync with God, but are now fallen. However, this seems to contradict a teaching of Jesus, who after founding his church stated that the "gates of Hell" would not prevail against it. This is taken to mean that his teaching would never be lost or corrupted, even if his followers are certainly less than perfect.

Another question I have concerning Jesus is the teaching that he was never crucified. It is said in the Qur'an that **"those who differ therein are full of conjecture,"** but I really can't help but wonder: there must have been witnesses to this crucifixion, and even non-Christian writers living during that time have written about the event.

I'm happy to have to this chance to speak with a Muslim about matters of our faiths and their history. I can't wait for your reply!
    -Chris

Email #03 – From: Ahmed Rashed
Sent: Monday, December 7, 2015 8:59 a.m.

In the Name of God; Most Gracious, Most Merciful:
    Good morning, Chris:
    I am happy that you have started the dialogue. I pray that I can be a resource for you. Our purpose at WhyIslam is to explain Islam in clear and plain language. Remember, it is only by asking and seeking answers that wisdom can be found. Now, on to your questions:
    1. The Islamic understanding is that the previous scriptures have a mix of some of what was originally revealed to

Moses and Jesus (peace be upon them) and much of what was added later by the "hands of the scribes." Muslims believe that the original Torah and Evangel were revealed by Almighty God. When Jesus (peace be upon him) began to call the Jews to return to sincere and devoted service to God, the Torah of Moses had already been subjected to serious instances of careless copying and dogmatic editing, but he confirmed in his preaching whatever remained intact of the divine revelation (see Matthew 5:17-18). So we see that the essence of the Torah was confirmed in the Evangel.

Six hundred years later, when the Evangel had suffered similar copying and editing, Muhammad resumed the Prophetic mission and confirmed whatever remained of both Torah and Evangel. He received from God the clarified book, the Qur'an, which would be protected forever from error and distortion. So it would serve as the protector and ultimate reference of all previous revelations. In a sense, the Qur'an is viewed as the Final Testament and therefore the final arbiter of what God truly intended to reveal to mankind. The Qur'an says about itself:

And We revealed to you the Book, with truth, confirming the Scripture that preceded it, and superseding it. So judge between them according to what God revealed, and do not follow their desires if they differ from the truth that has come to you. For each of you We have assigned a law and a method. Had God willed, He could have made you a single nation, but He tests you through what He has given you. So compete in righteousness. To God is your return, all of you; then He will inform you of what you had disputed. (5:48)

For this reason, whatever agrees with the Qur'an — like the verses that show Jesus did not claim partnership or identity with God (John 14:2, 28; Mark 12:29, 13:32; Luke 23:46; Matthew 12:18; Acts 3:13, 4:27) — we judge it as a portion of what was originally revealed by God.

And whatever disagrees with the Qur'an — like the idea that Jesus did claim partnership or identity with God or that he claimed that his teachings would not be lost or corrupted — we judge is as a portion of what was either misrepresented or dogmatically edited by men. Remember, there were many books and writings attributed to Jesus in the early centuries following Jesus's ascension. Many of those books were burned as heretical, and the early church leaders did not agree on what was actually Bible canon until the 3rd century CE. So Islam does not contradict the teachings of Jesus (peace be upon him); rather, it challenges whether the words in the Bible as written by the church are *actually* the words that Jesus himself (peace be upon him) said.

2. As for the crucifixion, let us take a look at what the Qur'an actually says:

And for their faithlessness, and their saying against Mary a monstrous slander.

And for their saying, "We have killed the Messiah, Jesus, the son of Mary, the Messenger of God." In fact, they did not kill him, nor did they crucify him, but it appeared to them as if they did. Indeed, those who differ about him are in doubt about it. They have no knowledge of it, except the following of assumptions. Certainly, they did not kill him.

Rather, God raised him up to Himself. God is Mighty and Wise.

There is none from the People of the Scripture but will believe in him before his death, and on the Day of Resurrection he will be a witness against them. (4:156-159)

The Bible indicates Jesus's (peace be upon him) prayers at Gethsemene went unanswered, even though he stayed up through the night crying and asking God, *"Let this cup pass from me, even so, Your will be done."* So rather than the "willing sacrificial lamb," it seems that Jesus (peace be upon him) did not want to be captured and was praying to God to protect and rescue him.

However, according to the Qur'an, Almighty God did answer his prayers. He did not go to the cross, but rather the likeness of him was put on another person who did go to the cross … so Almighty God did save Jesus, peace be upon him, from his enemies. Muslims believe he was raised up to God, and he will return in the Last Days to lead the true believers to victory over the Anti-Christ's armies.

Now you ask what evidence do we have for this, but you have missed the subtlety of God's rescue. God allowed the plan of Herod and his Roman allies to "appear" successful to them. The sequence of events is not refuted, rather the identity of the man on the cross is refuted. On the one hand, that would explain the sudden disappearance of Judas (his death is not eyewitnessed or agreed upon by the four canonical gospel accounts). On the other hand, it would explain how a Prophet of God could ever utter the complaint, *"My God, my God! Why have thou forsaken me!?"* God says in the Qur'an that the people who disagree about it — referring to the early church fathers who were debating about the nature of Jesus — are in doubt thereof; they have no knowledge of it except conjecture.

Apologies for the long-winded email, but the topics are important enough to warrant a comprehensive approach. Looking forward to your response and to continuing the dialogue!

May peace be with you,
Ahmed

Email #04 – From: Chris
Sent: Monday, December 7, 2015 11:32 a.m.

Greetings Ahmed!

There is no need to apologize for long-winded emails, I want the most comprehensive answers that I can find!

You seem very knowledgeable, so I feel that I can trust you with questions I find dubious from other sources, such as about scriptural corruption. I would like to know how we know the Qur'an is protected from the "hands of the Scribes." I understand that sending a new Prophet is the method through which God protects His teachings, so even though the Torah and Evangel became corrupt, they were only books on their own anyway, and God protected what they originally taught through later revelations. I hope you understand what I'm saying. But what can make us sure that there isn't anything added to or taken away from the Qur'an?

Concerning Jesus, not really being as "a lamb led to the slaughter, not making a sound," I will say that being afraid and being willing are not the same. In his prayer, Jesus prayed that the cup be taken from him, but in the end, Thy will be done. If God wanted him crucified, then how can we say that this prayer that His will be done went unanswered? Going through with God's will and asking it be done, even through a fear that causes bloody sweat, is a mark of true holiness, wouldn't you agree? Concerning his words on the cross, *"Why has Thou forsaken me,"* seems to be a reference to Psalm 22, which starts with these words and goes on to talk about how the Lord hasn't turned away and abhors not the affliction of the afflicted. In fact, the crucifixion follows the events described in the Psalm. Indeed, when he says this from the cross, those watching said, *"He is calling for Elijah,"* and when someone was going to give a drink from a sponge, they said, *"Wait! Let us see if Elijah will come for him."* So it would seem that the reference was understood by the bystanders.

Of course, all of that may be conjecture. No? If so, how do you tell?

I eagerly await your response! I hope it will be most long-winded, informative, and divinely inspired.

-Chris

Email #05 – From: Ahmed Rashed
Sent: Friday, December 11, 2015 3:17 p.m.

In the Name of God; Most Gracious, Most Merciful:

Good afternoon, Chris:

These are good questions, my friend. Let us take each one separately.

PART 1 - How was the Qur'an preserved?

During the Prophet's life, the Qur'an was revealed over a period of twenty-three years. Each revelation brought a new passage of the Qur'an. Some passages were only a few verses long; some were entire chapters. After each revelation, the Prophet (pbuh) would recite it to his Companions, and they memorized it or wrote it down. One of the Prophet's scribes, Zaid bin Thabit, reported that he used to write as the Prophet told him and then read back to the Prophet to make sure it was written correctly. It is important to note that Zaid was only one of the Prophet's scribes; Muslim scholars identify thirty-seven or thirty-eight other Companions who wrote down new revelations from directly from the Prophet, some more than others. Zaid and many of the early Muslims memorized the Qur'an immediately after the verses were revealed.

Those who memorized or wrote the new revelation from the Prophet would teach it to the rest of the community. Since the five daily prayers required a person to recite from what he knew of the Qur'an, memorization was encouraged and reinforced.

When the Prophet died, many Companions had memorized the entire Qur'an by heart, and many more had memorized large portions of it. Shortly after the death of the Prophet (within two years), Umar ibn Al-Khattab suggested to the first Caliph, Abu Bakr, that the Qur'an be compiled into one volume. Up until then, the Qur'an was written down in sections in the order they were revealed. A committee was formed under Zaid bin Thabit to gather the scattered material of the Qur'an into one volume. Great care was taken to compile the Qur'an exactly as it had been recited during the time of the Prophet.

To ensure this, Zaid first checked that each verse matched his memorization of the Qur'an. Second, each verse had to match the memories of two other Companions who had memorized the verse directly from the Prophet himself.

Finally, each verse had to match what the scribes had first written down under the direct supervision of the Prophet. Only verses that met all these criteria were included in the codex. This copy was kept with one of the widows of the Prophet, and it was available for anyone who wanted to reference it. When Umar became the second Caliph, many schools were established for the teaching of the Qur'an throughout the Muslim territories. One such school in Damascus had a total of 1,600 students who memorized the Qur'an under the instruction of Abu Dardaa, a well-known Companion of the Prophet who had memorized the entire Qur'an by heart.

As the Muslim Empire expanded, people in various places recited the Qur'an in their local dialect, and there arose the possibility of confusion and misunderstanding. To avoid this, the third Caliph, Uthman, ordered the preparation of standard copies of the Qur'an to be written in the dialect of the tribe of Quraysh. Prophet Muhammad was from the Quraysh tribe, so it was felt that this was the right dialect for the recitation of the Qur'an. Zaid bin Thabit (who was still alive and well at the time) was asked to prepare standard copies of the official manuscript with the help of Abdullah ibn Az-Zubair, Sa'id ibn Al-Aas, and Abdur-Rahman ibn Al-Harith, three Companions who had memorized the entire Qur'an. These standard copies were then sent to different parts of the Islamic State with a teacher to instruct how to recite the Qur'an correctly. All subsequent copies of the Qur'an had to conform to this standard Qur'an. This occurred approximately nineteen years after the death of the Prophet (seventeen years after the collection of the first codex). Many of the major Companions were still alive. Any of them could have raised objection if the text of these copies differed from what they learned from the Prophet. NOT A SINGLE ONE of the Companions who had memorized the entire Qur'an voiced any issues or errors with Uthman's standard Qur'an.

In fact, two original copies of Uthman's standard Qur'ans still exist today: one in the Topkapı Museum in Istanbul, Turkey, and the other in Tashkent, Uzbekistan.

PART 2 - Jesus on the cross?

So first we have to remember the primary reason why a Muslim denies that Jesus (peace be upon him) himself was crucified is because the Qur'an (which Muslims believe to be the literal word of God dictated to Muhammad) makes this claim. The analysis of Judas and the words of Jesus as represented in the New Testament is only *one* of the opinions of Muslim scholars. Since there is no authentic text from the Qur'an or the sayings of the Prophet to determine what really happened, this is called only a theory by Islamic scholars, and they always conclude, "And God knows best."

Having said that, let us zoom out our view and consider what is really going on here. One book claims that Jesus (peace be upon him) was crucified; the other claims he was not. These are two competing truth-claims that both traditions believe to be from God. How do we reconcile the representation of Jesus (pbuh) in the Qur'an with that in the Bible? I believe we have to look into what is it that Jesus (pbuh) meant to convey to his listeners. Is Jesus (pbuh) a Prophet like all other prophets sent by God, or is he something different? Did he preach a Concept of God and Way of Salvation that was *radically different* from the prophets that came before, or did he preach *a continuation of their message*?

Most Christians would choose *radically different*, since he changed the rules for achieving salvation. All Muslims would choose *a continuation of their message*, that he preached just what all the previous prophets preached. Muslims believe it is only his followers who came after, especially Paul, whose teachings overshadowed and altered the crux of what Jesus actually preached during his mission. Many people (including Christians) are already well aware of the tension between Christ's teachings and those of Paul. Mainstream Christianity tries to harmonize the two. There are Protestants called dispensationalists who see the clear-cut division between Jesus and Paul's teaching but attribute this to a change in the economy of salvation and emphasize Paul's role for today's church.

What if we put Pauline doctrines aside? What if we only looked at the most reliable sayings and quotations of Jesus (pbuh)? How would that compare with what the Qur'an says? Many Christians have done this exercise, and they admit that if you only go by the most authentic sayings attributed to Jesus — the famous "Q" verses or the "Historical Jesus" — then the Qur'anic picture of Jesus (pbuh) is a pretty good match to those authentic sayings.

In this light, the vista opens up to see a pattern of God's revelation that is consistent from Adam to Abraham and Moses all the way through to Jesus and Muhammad (peace be upon them all). Even though there are differences (slight changes in dietary habits, different holy day, etc.), there is even greater consistency in the glorification of the one true God.

That's my long-winded essay for this week. Looking forward to your reply!

May peace be with you,
Ahmed

Email #06 – From: Chris
Sent: Friday, December 11, 2015 11:27 p.m.

Hello Ahmed!

I'm so glad to hear from you again! I was actually beginning to worry.

It's interesting to hear that there are original copies of the Qur'an. Knowing those exist, along with the zeal of Zaid and others, I'm sure the Qur'an has not suffered corruption, at least not in Arabic. I have heard that some translations differ, especially the Reformist. The very nice Qur'an I received in the mail is the Yusuf Ali. I wonder if this one would be your recommendation.

You should know that Catholics are certainly not dispensationlists. I have never heard of this before now, but I'm not surprised that it exists. Protestants are known to come up with all sorts of odd doctrines and histories. Just look at Mormonism and the Jehovah's Witnesses!

That being said, I'm not aware of anything Paul said that contradicts any saying of Jesus. As a Muslim looking at these things, I wonder if you could point some out for me. Also, how has Jesus changed the rules for achieving salvation? I know it seems like these are things that I should already know, but I am slow to learn… Or at least slow to realization.

I feel like the viewpoint you have brought up will be very interesting to explore. I can't wait for your reply!

-Chris

Email #07 – From: Ahmed Rashed
Sent: Tuesday, December 22, 2015 10:08 a.m.

In the Name of God; Most Gracious, Most Merciful:
    Hello Chris!

    I am so so sorry for the long delay in my reply. My father-in-law had a series of doctor appointments. Please forgive me.

    To proceed, regarding the Qur'an translation; I do not like Yusuf Ali because there are interpretive issues in it (word choices and explanations) that are not orthodox for some of the more esoteric verses. This is okay for most students, but I prefer *Oxford Classics* "The Qur'an" by MAS Haleem or the Saheeh-International translations. The Saheeh-International is more literally faithful to the original Arabic, while the MAS Haleem translation has more flowing English word order and sentence structure.

    As for the Jesus vs. Paul difference, a little background is in order. The Gospel of Mark, most Christian scholars believe, is the oldest extant gospel. Interestingly, Matthew and Luke depend on Mark for much, but not all, of their material. The Gospel of John does not depend on any other gospel in a textual sense; it is independent in a way that the other three gospels are not. It was also compiled later than the others.

    If we remove the influence of Mark and look at what Matthew and Luke still have in common, we find dozens of obviously parallel verses in Matthew and Luke — verses that often give nearly verbatim expressions of the same saying.

    Many scholars feel these parallel verses constitute clear evidence of a "sayings gospel" that supplies Matthew and Luke with substantial content. These parallel verses are known as Q verses, and they appear to reflect a lost manuscript that many believe is older than even Mark's Gospel.

    The whole point of this idea is that the authors of Matthew and Luke used two written sources — Mark and the Q verses — in developing their own accounts of the life of Jesus. For more details on this, check out *The Complete Gospels*, edited by Robert J. Miller (Harper, 1992).

Anyway, traditionalist Christian clergy and theologians are generally hostile to the Q verses. The reason is that the Q verses portray Jesus as a distinctly human prophet, undermining Paul's doctrine of the Trinity. Q verses also tend to confirm the claim that surviving scriptures of Christianity have been tampered with in a way meant to dilute rigorous monotheism and promote formulations such as "Father, Son, and Holy Spirit."

It is important to note that Q scholars are Christian scholars researching the origins and authenticity of their scriptures, not Muslims or atheists trying to undermine Christianity. To put it simply, today's best New Testament experts believe that **some** Gospel verses appear to present a *more historically accurate* picture of Jesus than **other** Gospel verses do.

What does this have to do with Paul, you might ask?

Well, Paul taught — just like C.S. Lewis and thousands of other great Christian thinkers tell us — that you and I can never, no matter how hard we may try, live up to the demands of God as He expects them to be fulfilled. For this reason, a redeemer is required to atone for the failings of man.

However, these Q verses show Jesus teaching a different message. Jesus explicitly rejects his own claims of divinity (Matthew 7:21 and Luke 4:8). Jesus refers to himself as the Son of Adam and the Son of Man. Jesus maintains that complete submission to the will of God, before death overtakes us and we are held accountable for our sins, is the criterion for salvation (Matthew 7:13-14 and Luke 10:26-28). The Q verses do not point to the idea of Jesus's divinity, his status as redeemer, or the requirement of atonement for salvation as Paul's various letters do.

This is what I meant by the disconnect between the earliest Gospel sources, the early sayings of Jesus (pbuh), and the later Books of the New Testament, specifically the Epistles of Paul.

Again, please forgive the long-winded email and forgive the delay in responding.

May peace be with you,
Ahmed

Email #08 – From: Chris
Sent: Tuesday, December 29, 2015 9:00 p.m.

Greetings Ahmed! I'm glad to hear from you again. I'm sorry about your father; I hope he's doing well. I'm also sorry about my own late reply, because of the holidays and all.

I must admit that I don't know much about the "Q" gospel. I have heard of it and doubt myself, though not necessarily for traditionalist reasons. No one seems to have even a fragment of it, and similarities between two gospels are the only evidence. Is it really so far-fetched to assume that four people witnessing the same things would write similar stories about it? Even without collaboration, they would still come out being similar.

In Matthew 7:21, I find what is actually one of my favorite verses. *"Not everyone who says to me, 'Lord, Lord' will enter into the kingdom of God, but only the one who does the will of my Father in heaven. They will say to me, 'Lord, did we not drive out demons, prophesy, and do mighty deeds in your name?'"* He says not everyone will enter the kingdom, but he didn't say that no one would. He seems to be accepting the title of Lord and the fact that good things were done in his name.

This is interesting, because in Luke 10:26-28, it reads, *"Jesus said to him, "What is written in the law? How do you read it?' He said to him in reply, 'You shall love the Lord, your God, with all your heart, and with all your being, with all your strength, and with all your mind, and your neighbor as yourself.' He replied to him, 'You have answered correctly, do this and you will live.'"* If Jesus is Lord, and loving the Lord is a requirement to live, then these verses and Paul would agree. After all, though we may disagree upon everything else, one thing I know we both agree on is that redemption and atonement come from God alone.

Please don't be sorry for long-winded emails. Like I said, the more exhaustive and long-winded, the better! I look forward to your reply.

-Chris

Email #09 – From: Ahmed Rashed
Sent: Tuesday, January 5, 2016 8:57 a.m.

In the Name of God; Most Gracious, Most Merciful:

Good morning, Chris:

I hope you had a nice vacation with your family and friends, God willing. I was out of town for most of the winter break, so I am now catching up on my emails.

This one won't be quite so long-winded…

Let us start with your last comment, redemption and atonement come from God alone. As you said, we both agree on this statement. Without going any further in the Q discussion or the Paul/Jesus discussion, suffice it to say that Muslims view the crucifixion as intrinsically unnecessary. Since God is the Most Gracious, the Oft-Repenting, the Forbearing, and Ever-Compassionate, Muslims believe He is willing and able to forgive sins, even the one committed by Adam and Eve. Therefore, Islam does not have Original Sin, and there is no need for a Universal redeemer for mankind. If there is no Original Sin, there is no need for a universal redeemer. In addition, this concept of God means that each human being can turn to God without any intermediate and ask for forgiveness. Since repentance is in the hands of each human being, the role of all prophets (including Jesus, in the Islamic worldview) is to remind people of God's mercy and exhort them to turn to God themselves. So in a sense, Muslims view that Jesus's role was to "help you get it together" rather than "get it together for you."

Now, as for the crucifixion act itself, the Qur'an advises (as discussed in my first email) that Jesus himself was not actually crucified, but rather it only appeared that he was. This addresses the historical context in the Islamic worldview.

May peace be with you,
Ahmed

Email #10 – From: Chris
Sent: Thursday, January 7, 2016 1:16 a.m.

Greetings Ahmed!

I bet you have a lot of emails. I wonder how many other discussions you're in the middle of right now. I probably can't even imagine!

I think I'm going to be long-winded this time. I need to say what I've been thinking about.

We both agree that God doesn't get it together for us. *"Behold, I stand at the door and knock, and whoever answers I will come in with him."* He won't open the door himself, of course. The saying means that we must be open to God and do as he says. I know many Protestants teach the idea of "once saved, always saved," but I will have none of that. That is VERY wrong, in my opinion.

Regarding this Muslim view of the crucifixion, I wonder if it's strictly taught that someone else was crucified in his place. That definitely seems to be the teaching, but I wonder if it can also be taught that the word "appearance" could be substituted for the word "seemed." If so, it could be taught that no crucifixion of any kind ever took place! What do you think? Also, on the matter of differences of the story in the Bible and the story in the Qur'an, there is a difference not only in his death, but in his birth! In Maryam, Mary had the child under a palm tree in the wilderness, whereas in the Gospels she had him in some kind of stable. There is also no star, as far as I know, nor the three Magi. I haven't read anything yet about the Massacre of the Holy Innocents, when Herod killed all those children looking for the child Jesus. I would like to hear your take on these differences and what Muslims believe of the birth of Jesus.

Maryam, from the Qur'an, was an interesting read. It lays down the logic of the Muslim belief of God not begetting a son. God only says, '"Be!" and it becomes, is what it asserts. It seems to teach that Isaac and John the Baptist were all created by God miraculously, and Adam directly! Yet they weren't part of a trinity of any kind, so what makes Jesus any different than Adam? Adam was without sin, yet he was not a person of God.

We Catholics believe Mary was conceived without sin, and yet we don't teach she is a goddess or a person of God (even though the Qur'an says we do). So it's not that he is a direct creation, nor is it that he was sinless. But God is the Self-Sustaining. He simply is, and if he visits us in the form of a divine humanity, that divinity would come from its own self. I can't say that God said, "Be!" because God always has been and because the Bible says that *"in the beginning was the Word."*

Whence, then, comes room for him to enter time in the form of a human? Is it odd to say that Christ is born, when he always was? Did he ever really die, since death marks the end of something, and God is eternal? The teaching for us here is that God's power was never limited in the flesh of Jesus. It's not that God's presence and power was constrained and contained in that place and time; after all, flesh can never contain God's glory. I can't say that God created the person of Jesus. But the Bible says that Jesus "grew in stature and wisdom," a thing that divinity does not do, but he is a divine person as the Son.

The teaching here is that his human and divine persons were not confused or separate but have a "hypostatic union," sometimes called a mystical union. But if he were human and divine, as one being and not two (or three), and his humanity and divinity were indeed one, I can't say that God created his humanity, because if his humanity and divinity were one, then his humanity must have already existed, along with the eternal divinity. To this, and I admit the further this paragraph goes, the more I doubt what I say is orthodox, I only have the old saying, *"As above, so below."* The Nicene Creed states that *"he was begotten, not made, one in being with the Father."* He is begotten, caused to be, as God causes Himself. The teaching — seems — to be that the Son, as God, was begotten, caused to be, in one order, and then, as a sign to us all, caused to be in another, for the sake of salvation. I've been thinking about all of that a lot more since I started talking to you.

But you say Islam doesn't teach Original Sin, so there is no need for a savior. Indeed, we agree that God can forgive any sin, even Original Sin. If Christ is God, then that crucifixion would not be just a sacrifice. If it were just a sacrifice of a man, it wouldn't have meant much. And the grace of baptism is the beginning of a life of being forgiven, even from Original Sin, so I perceive no difficulty with our teaching of God's total and unrestrained offering of forgiveness to us, as we only need to be open, be truly repentant and do as He says, and forgiveness comes.

But what's Original Sin anyway? It's called an inheritance, so it's not something that we do. It seems to be that it's Adam's sin that he turned away. He had God's grace for the fact that he was created by God and in His image, and we were supposed to receive it from him as his descendants. He had that grace as part of his nature, given by God. When Adam turned away, he lost that grace and so damaged his human nature, and we, as his descendants, assumed this broken nature, as humans like him. And so we must turn to God to give us His grace.

Hence the Christian need for the crucifixion. It's written that we must attach ourselves to him, "like a branch grafted to the tree," attaching ourselves to his perfect humanity and sharing in his grace. Thus becoming the Jewish Messiah. But I bet you knew how that's supposed to work already.

I actually have a theory about about a pattern in the Old Testament, how the firstborn gets an automatic blessing, forfeits it, and the secondborn becomes a prophet by receiving the blessing that was taken away, but I've gotten quite long-winded as it is. So I have to ask, DOES this definition of Original Sin contradict Islamic teaching?

The Qur'an definitely has a unique writing style. I hope I didn't get the point of Maryam totally wrong, but the emphasis certainly seemed to be on God's ability to create from nothing. What do you think? I've given you a good bit of my thoughts. I really want to hear your own. I bet you think a lot about this too.

Still hope your father is well.
-Chris

Email #11 – From: Ahmed Rashed
Sent: Thursday, January 14, 2016 1:44 p.m.

In the Name of God; Most Gracious, Most Merciful:

Good afternoon, Chris:

Regarding the Muslim view of crucifixion, what is taught is what is written in the Qur'an: it only appeared to the enemies of Christ that he was crucified. Whether it was another person, a simulacrum, or just an illusion is not discussed. Since the Prophet warned us about speculating about that which is Unseen and on which no divine revelation has been sent to clarify, Muslim scholars to this day have stopped their discussions at this point.

As for Mary, you are correct about the differences in birthplace and visitors and signs. While there is no record in the Qur'an or the sayings of the Prophet that Mary was visited by Magi and a star shown in the sky, Muslim scholars point out that the Qur'an usually does not give these kind of details anyway. Therefore, since these events do not contradict the storyline of the Qur'an, Muslim scholars conclude we may accept those Biblical episodes or not accept them, and either choice is fine. However, since the Qur'an explicitly mentions Mary withdrawing away from her community to avoid any scandal of her being pregnant and explicitly mentions her giving birth under a date palm tree, Muslims take this a fact and conclude that the Biblical storyline is in error.

Moving to the next point, I am glad you found Maryam to be an interesting read, because it does as you say lay down the logic of Muslim belief regarding Jesus. It is not quite right to say that Isaac and John were born miraculously in the sense that God said "be," and it is. Rather, God allowed two women who were barren and infertile to become fertile to conceive in the "usual" way with their respective husbands. Yes, it is God's command that made the infertile fertile (even if only for one time), but it is not quite the same level of miracle as the act of creating Jesus *ex nihilo* in the womb of Mary.

Also, I checked the translation again, and it does not say that Muslims believe Christians teach Mary is a person of God; rather it says: **And behold! God will say: "O Jesus the son of Mary! Didst thou say unto men, worship me and my mother as deities beside of God?" (5:116)**

The word translated as "deities" does not just mean "gods"; it means any object of supplication. So while it is true that most Christians do not worship Mary, my own discussions with Catholics and other kinds of Christians show that some Christians DO call upon Mary for certain prayers or supplications. That is the nuanced meaning that the Qur'an is admonishing here. In Islam it is forbidden to supplicate to any angel, prophet, pious person, or anything or anybody other than God.

Now we come to the meat of your message: how is Jesus divine and how is he human? If he is human and created by the divine, then why consider him a person in divinity? This is the question the Qur'an poses. As you yourself admitted, as you try to explain the concept of Jesus's divinity, you find yourself unsure whether you are saying something orthodox or not. The Nicene Creed was written over 350 years after Christ's ascension, and it is a known fact that there were several weeks of debate among the Christian leaders before they could agree on its formulation. It seems remarkable that over ten generations would pass before the followers of Jesus could understand his message.

This is the core of the Qur'an's message. It claims (and some accept and some reject the claim) that the idea of Jesus having some part of divinity is an idea that DID NOT originate from Jesus himself.

Which brings us to the question of why anyone would claim Jesus to be divine anyway. This is the issue of Original Sin. If Jesus did NOT have divinity, then his sacrifice would not be sufficient to atone or redeem humanity. But why is this so? Why is sacrifice of Person J required to atone for the sin of Person A and all of Person A's descendants? Islam clearly and emphatically rejects the concept of inherited sin.

The Prophet said, "Allah, the Exalted and Glorious, has said: 'I live in the thought of My servant and I am with him as he remembers Me.'"

The Prophet also said, "Allah, the Exalted and Glorious, has said: 'When My servant draws near to Me by the span of his hand, I draw near him by the length of a cubit. When he draws near to Me by the length of a cubit, I draw near him by the length of a fathom. When he draws near to Me walking, I draw close to him hurriedly."

And: "Verily, when the believer commits a sin, a black spot appears upon his heart. If he repents and abandons the sin and seeks forgiveness, then his heart will be polished. If he increases in sin, then the blackness is increased."

In the Qur'an, God says, **But indeed, I am the Perpetual Forgiver of whoever repents and believes and does righteousness and then continues in guidance. (20:82)**

Also, the Qur'an says in 6:164, 17:15, 35:18, 39:7, and 53:38 that "…NO bearer of burdens (meaning sins) shall be made to bear another's burden…"

So these are just a few verses (and there are many more) that teach that every human being can TURN BACK to God on their own, with their own actions, without the need (or even the option) of an intermediary savior or redeemer. In fact, the Qur'an (2:30-36) describes that this is exactly what happened with Adam. The Qur'an teaches that Adam did not *turn away*, but rather he was tricked, tempted, and made a mistake, but then he and Eve recognized their error and repented to God and were forgiven. All this before God commanded them to go down to Earth. This is very major difference from the Biblical narrative … the idea that Adam turned back and sought repentance and was GRANTED that repentance before leaving Heaven undermines much of the story that Christianity paints.

Therefore, the Christian definition of Original Sin does in fact contradict Islamic teachings. Just as the Islamic teachings on Sin and Salvation do in fact contradict Christian teachings. These are irreconcilable theologies, and this is something that mature scholars of both traditions have agreed upon.

Sorry for responding so late, my friend, but I like to give your points the time and attention they deserve for a reply. Looking forward to continuing the discussion!

May peace be with you,
Ahmed

Email #12 – From: Chris
Sent: Saturday, January 16, 2016 12:32 a.m.

Hello Ahmed!

Well, I suppose I'll get right to it.

About Maryam. I mean, it used the word "worship," though. I suppose, if I may argue against myself, that having an object of supplication other than God would imply some kind of worship. If Mary is in Heaven praying, wouldn't she already be praying for the whole world? And it's not like Mary has power over anything or can help us without God's leave, so God should be our sole source of supplication. But do Muslims ask other Muslims to remember them in their prayers? I know that prayer isn't for granting wishes as much as it is communicating your heartfelt desire for God's mercy, love, and guidance, but is it okay to ask for favors too and ask other Muslims to remember their needs?

Anyway, I know there was a group of Christians at that time who did, in fact, worship Mary. It could be talking about this sect.

On the subject of the fall of Adam and glorification of Jesus, this is where my understanding is exhausted. I get how it works. Adam is the first human, so like when the first diamond ever appeared, it defined the nature of every diamond after it. The existence of "diamond" has been defined. So it was with man. Adam defined the nature of humanity, and he had grace but fell. The existence of "human" has been defined as such.

But Jesus was different. In order to pull humanity out of this nature, Jesus was sent as a "new Adam." Given a spotless humanity from his mother by power of Divinity from God, he could be human without Adam's nature. "Grafting ourselves like a branch to the tree," we grow with him in this nature and "become a new creation," "for we are convinced that because one has died for all, so all have died." These two two Corinthians quotes make me believe my understanding isn't far off.

But you say that there is no bearer of sins. Maybe not in the sense of responsibility. It's not that God is punishing us for the sin of Adam. We are suffering the consequence of his sin. In my church, it is taught that while the spiritual consequences of sin are forgiven, the physical, natural consequences remain (except in certain situations). So Original Sin is the sin of Adam, the stain it leaves is the mark he left of the nature of humanity, and concupisence, which is a leaning towards sin, is the natural consequence.

The Christian story does not have Adam repenting. Instead, when confronted by God about what he had done, he blamed Eve, and Eve blamed Satan. One might assume he never repented. God removed him from Eden so that he wouldn't eat of the Tree of Life and live forever — a thing he can't do in his fallen state.

But in Islam, the story goes that he realized what he did, and repented. Adam only committed a mistake. I had to do a little searching to find the difference between a "mistake" and a sin. It would seem that because Adam had never before encountered evil, he didn't know anything about it when he was tempted by Satan.

He was taken advantage of. I think I get it. It's like the old saying, "Fool me once, shame on you." But now humans have learned sin and how to recognize the whispers of Satan. We would be held responsible for falling into his lies now, because the saying continues, "Fool me twice, shame on me." So we can't blame Adam in Islam for passing on a broken nature. Even if the nature was broken, God repaired it. But in Islam, this fall was anticipated by God. The threat of the fall was human to begin with. The angels seemed to see it coming as well. I wonder if it can be said that we are still, as humanity, in the process of creation?

So did I get it right? I found some other tidbits too. Is it true you worship on Friday because that was the day that Adam was created? You know, that is the sixth day. It is a number — very — frowned upon in both Judaism and Christianity. Apparently, it seems to mean a lack of divine completeness and perfection, as God "rested" on the seventh.

I can't wait to hear from you.

-Chris

Email #13 – From: Ahmed Rashed
Sent: Tuesday, January 19, 2016 9:04 a.m.

In the Name of God; Most Gracious, Most Merciful:

Good morning, Chris!

First, I would like to apologize for being so terse in my last email. I was feeling guilty that I had taken so long to respond to you that I just started writing, trying to get all my ideas down before I forgot them or got pulled away to other issues. Please forgive me. I will try to be more conversational from now on.

Your conversations are always thoughtful, so I feel they deserve a good, thoughtful engagement. Reflecting about Mary (Maryam), worship and supplication are closely connected in Islam, which is why it is a sensitive topic. However, there IS a difference between praying FOR someone vs. praying TO someone. Praying for someone is allowed and encouraged in Islam, so asking a person to remember you in their prayers is common among Muslims. However, praying TO the Prophet, or a sheikh, or an angel, or a dead ancestor (no matter how pious) is crossing the line. I agree that it is possible that the verse in the Qur'an is referencing a sect that actually worshiped Mary, but since I am not familiar with the in-depth interpretation of that passage, I cannot say for sure.

On the subject of Adam and Jesus, you are right that this is the crux of the matter between the Islamic and Christian concepts of God, human nature, sin, and salvation. Let us start with this passage from the Qur'an:

Sura 2

30. When your Lord said to the angels, "I am placing a successor on earth." They said, "Will You place in it someone who will cause corruption and shed blood, while we praise and sanctify You?" He said, "I know what you do not know."

31. And He taught Adam the names, all of them; then he presented them to the angels, and said, "Tell Me the names of these, if you are sincere."

32. They said, "Glory be to You! We have no knowledge except what You have taught us. It is you who are the Knowledgeable, the Wise."

33. He said, "O Adam, tell them their names." And when he told them their names, He said, "Did I not tell you that I know the secrets of the heavens and the earth, and that I know what you reveal and what you conceal?"

34. And We said to the angels, "Bow down to Adam." They bowed down, except for Satan. He refused, was arrogant, and was one of the disbelievers.

35. We said, "O Adam, inhabit the Garden, you and your spouse, and eat from it freely as you please, but do not approach this tree, lest you become wrongdoers."

36. But Satan caused them to slip from it, and caused them to depart the state they were in. We said, "Go down, some of you enemies of one another. And you will have residence on earth, and enjoyment for a while."

37. Then Adam received words from his Lord, so He relented towards him. He is the Relenting, the Merciful.

38. We said, "Go down from it, all of you. Yet whenever guidance comes to you from Me, then whoever follows My guidance-they have nothing to fear, nor shall they grieve.

39. But those who disbelieve and reject Our signs — these are the inmates of the Fire — wherein they will remain forever."

So from this we see that God intended Adam and his progeny to live on EARTH. We also see that the angels understood the nature of Adam's free will and that it would lead to corruption and bloodshed. God's reply points to the fact that He knew this already, but there are other reasons why only He knows for carrying out His plan. This story is told from a slightly different angle in the Qur'an 7:11-24 and 15:26-50. Another passage of the Qur'an that is interesting to look at is the following:

Sura 20

115. And We made a Covenant with Adam before, but he forgot, and We found in him no resolve.

116. And when We said to the angels, "Bow down to Adam." They bowed down, except for Satan; he refused.

117. We said, "O Adam, this is an enemy to you and to your wife. So do not let him make you leave the Garden, for then you will suffer.

118. In it you will never go hungry, nor be naked.

119. Nor will you be thirsty in it, nor will you swelter."

120. But Satan whispered to him. He said, "O Adam, shall I show you the Tree of Immortality, and a kingdom that never decays?"

121. And so they ate from it; whereupon their bodies became visible to them, and they started covering themselves with the leaves of the Garden. Thus Adam disobeyed his Lord, and fell.

122. But then his Lord recalled him, and pardoned him, and guided him.

123. He said, "Go down from it, altogether; some of you enemies of some others. But whenever guidance comes to you from Me, whoever follows My guidance, will not go astray, nor suffer.

124. But whoever turns away from My Reminder, for him is a confined life. And We will raise him on the Day of Resurrection blind."

Especially notice 121-122: the Qur'an states that Adam certainly disobeyed and fell but that God recalled him, forgave him, and guided him. All these passages point out to a fundamental difference between the Biblical and Qur'anic narrative: is the nature of Adam's and humanity's mistakes, sins, and transgressions based on a nature that needs *overhaul and redemption* or a nature that needs *guidance and reform*? The Bible points to the former, while the Qur'an points to the latter.

The reality was that Adam did not have any experience with the whisperings and ploys of Satan. Adam had seen the arrogance of Satan when he refused to follow the commands of God; he knew that Satan was his enemy but had no familiarity with how to resist Satan's tricks and schemes.

God tested Adam so that he could learn and gain experience. In this way God prepared Adam for his role on Earth as a caretaker and a Prophet of God. From this experience, Adam learned the great lesson that Satan is cunning, ungrateful, and the avowed enemy of mankind. Adam, Eve and their descendants learned that Satan caused their expulsion from Heaven. Obedience to God and enmity toward Satan is the only path back to Heaven.

The Qur'an tells us that Adam subsequently received from his Lord some words: a supplication to pray, which invoked God's forgiveness. This experience was an essential lesson and demonstrated free will. If Adam and Eve were to live on Earth, they needed to be aware of the tricks and schemes of Satan, they also needed to understand the dire consequences of sin, and the infinite mercy and forgiveness of God. God knew that Adam and Eve would eat from the tree. He knew that Satan would strip away their innocence.

This is the context and backstory for the entire drama of human existence on Earth. Islam teaches that human nature is intrinsically good (not broken) but in need of guidance and continual maintenance (i.e., reconnecting to God regularly).

So you got it mostly right, Chris. As for the idea that "humanity is in the process of creation," I would reply that Islam teaches that each human heart or soul is in the process of "cultivating a relationship with its Creator." So the physical creation is "done" for the most part, but the spiritual development starts at birth and continues until death. The person who uses that time wisely for cultivating his soul and connecting with his

Creator will be successful in the hereafter, whereas those who neglect or corrupt their soul and ignore their Creator will be ruined in the hereafter. That is enough for now, I think; there are many talking points to touch on. Looking forward to your reply.

May peace be with you,
Ahmed

Email #14 – From: Chris
Sent: Sunday, February 14, 2016 9:38 p.m.

Ahmed! It's my turn to apologize to you! To be honest, I was the one worried about being terse in all of my emails. Now look at me! It has taken me almost a month to get back to you. I am sorry for that, and thank you for the time you take to think about these things.

If I may state a few observations, the story according to Islam seems to imply that humans are higher than angels and that angels lack free will. I'm sure you know that it is the opposite in Christianity. In fact, Satan was once the highest of angels who fell and became the lowest of all creation. Kind of like that saying, "The bigger they are, the harder they fall." Or perhaps in more Biblical language, the closer you are to God, the stricter the punishment for falling away, and you seem to yield a punishment relative to the place God has for you. Hence, Satan became the evil one, the most contemptible, yet still no match for God.

So angels are higher, being closer to God than us, and then us, and then demons, who are angels that fell with Satan, once called Lucifer.

In Islam, though, I understand that Satan was a jinn named Iblis. The jinn are human-like spirits who also have free will. It would seem that humans are above not only angels but also jinn, because he knew the "names," and not because he had free will. I have never understood this. I always draw a blank. Whose names was he taught? And how does knowing these names place him above the angels? Do you know the names? I don't suppose Islam would say that I know the names…

If I may make another observation, Sura 20:120 is very interesting to me. You may recall that in the Biblical Eden, there were two trees: the Tree of the Knowledge of Good and Evil, and the Tree of Life, which granted immortality. Here, though, it seems there was only the Tree of Good and Evil, which Satan tricked Adam into believing was a Tree of Immortality, and a kingdom which does not decay. This is reminiscent of the temptations of Jesus, one of which was the Satan promised Jesus the whole world and all of its kingdoms if he worshipped him.

Anyway, regarding human nature, we seem to almost agree. If I may quote Hebrews 1:1-2, *"In times past, God spoke in partial and various ways to our ancestors through the Prophets; in these last days he has spoken to us through a son, whom he made heir of all things and through whom he created the universe."* (NABRE).

We also believe that human nature is intrinsically good but in need of guidance and reform. Not just guidance by itself, because like the saying goes, "You can lead a horse to water, but you can't make him drink," and not just reform by itself because clay needs guiding hands to find its shape. The difference between our faiths, it seems, is that Christians believe in a sort of process of guidance. Again, to quote Hebrews, which quotes Jeremiah 31:31-34:

"Behold, the days are coming, says the Lord, when I will conclude a new covenant with the house of Israel and the house of Judah. It will not be like the covenant I made with their fathers the day I took them by the hand to lead them forth from the land of Egypt; for they did not stand by my covenant and I ignored them, says the Lord: I will put my laws in their minds and I will write them upon their hearts. I will be their God and they shall be my people. And they shall not teach, each one his fellow citizen and kinsman, saying, "Know the Lord" for all shall know me, from least to greatest. For I will forgive their evildoing and remember their sins no more."

God guided his people in preparation for a final covenant, which would completely fulfill and complete the law. So He spoke in "partial and various ways" to them.

However, I understand that Islam teaches that the Islam as preached by Muhammad is the same as the Islam preached by Abraham. So could one say that the guidance of Islam has never been partial and that it is the same now as it was in the beginning?

Again, I'm so sorry for taking so long to reply. I hope you've been well.

-Chris

Email #15 – From: Ahmed Rashed
Sent: Friday, February 19, 2016 8:45 a.m.

In the Name of God; Most Gracious, Most Merciful:

Good morning, Chris:

It is good to hear from you again. Don't worry about taking so long to reply. God knows how busy we both are, so it is understandable with these deep discussions that it may take a few days for either of us to sit down and compose a message.

To proceed, your initial observations are correct. The Islamic view of angels and demons (devils) is opposite of that in Christianity. Christianity teaches that angels and demons are flip sides of the same creation (good are called angels and evil are called demons or devils), whereas Islam teaches that angels are a distinct creation that have a fixed status with God due to their lack of free will. Islam teaches that humans and jinn (demons) are two other separate creations that have free will and therefore both can be either good or evil. In the Qur'an, both humans and jinn who are evil and tempt or seduce others to evil are called devils.

It is true that the "the bigger they are, the harder they fall," which is why the Qur'an highlights stories of "pious" people who were seriously punished when they fell to temptation and turned to evil. Satan is just one example of this. He was the "best" of the jinn when they had stewardship of the Earth, and that is why he was elevated to the company of the angels. However, he failed his final test when God created Adam and commanded the angelic company to bow down out of honor and respect. Satan became arrogant and refused this order; therefore, God cursed him and was about to cast him out. When Satan asked God for respite, God granted it to him and then warned Adam and his wife that Satan was an enemy of them both, so they should beware of him. However, Satan still succeeded in tempting them to eat of the forbidden tree.

Getting back to the second point about Adam being closer to God than the angels or the jinn, there is a small clarification: the angels have a fixed status with God due to their inability to disobey Him. Humans and jinn have a variable status. Most are worse than angels, because most have less reverence and fear and knowledge of God than the angels. However, both human and jinn have the POTENTIAL to be closer to God than the angels, and that is by piety and good deeds. So it is a latent superiority, not intrinsic. As for the humans being superior to jinn, this is a topic of discussion and speculation among Muslim scholars. Some suggest that the fact that Satan himself was elevated to the company of angels points to the conclusion that even jinn can achieve high status with God. Others point out that humans are above jinn because God asked the angels and the "best" jinn to honer Adam. However, these arguments are about two singular representatives of these species (Adam for humans and Iblis for jinn)... So even if the "best" human is better than the "best" jinn in the eyes of God, it certainly is not the case that all humans are better than all jinn. There will certainly be individual jinns who are more pious than individual humans and therefore achieve a higher status and perhaps even surpass the ranks of the angels. God accounts for everything, and nothing goes unnoticed or unrewarded.

As for "knowing the names," remember the context of this passage. It is relating the discussion between God and His angels before the creation of Adam but after the creation of jinn. This is how the angels know that corruption accompany free will.

A quick definition — *Khalifah*: one who exercises the delegated powers on behalf of another as his vicegerent. *Khalifah* thus is not the master but rather deputy of the master; his powers are not his own but delegated to him by the real master.

From the word *Khalifah* they had understood that the one who was about to be created was going to be entrusted with some powers, but they could not understand how an autonomous creature could fit in this totalitarian system of the universe. They also could not understand how that part of the universe, in which someone was entrusted with autonomy, could be free from disorder. They simply meant to say, "We are carrying out orders obediently, faithfully, and earnestly and are keeping the whole universe clean and in order, and sing hymns of Your praise and sanctify You as Your humble servants. Therefore, we are unable to understand what need then is there for a vicegerent."

God's response was basically, "You can not understand the need and wisdom of the appointment of a vicegerent as I do. Your services do not suffice for the purpose that I have in view. I want something more than the services you have mentioned. That is why I am going to create a being on the Earth and endow him with some powers."

Naming is the means by which the human mind grasps the knowledge of things. Hence, the whole information of man, in fact, consists of assigning names for things. Thus, teaching Adam the names of all things was meant to impart knowledge to him.

Muslim scholars speculate that the knowledge of each angel and of each species of angels is confined only to his or its own special sphere. For example, the angels who deal with the air know everything about the air but nothing about water. The same is true about the angels who are responsible for other spheres. In contrast to them, man has been granted comprehensive knowledge. He may not know as much about these things as the angels in charge of a special sphere do, but the comprehensiveness of knowledge that man has been granted has not been granted to the angels. It is this innate curiosity and intellectual capacity that God showcased to the angels to respond to their concerns.

In a way, God informed them, "I am not giving Adam only authority but also knowledge. The chaos that you apprehended from his appointment is only one aspect of the matter. It has its good aspect also, which is more weighty and valuable than the evil aspect, and a wise man does not give up a greater good because of a lesser evil."

As for your observation of 20:120, yes the Qur'an mentions a single forbidden tree, not different ones like the Bible. There is also another subtle difference that Muslim scholars and mystics point out to astute students: in the Qur'an, Satan flat-out LIES to Adam and Eve. The tree that God forbidden did not have any special powers. The tree was a test from God. The act of DISOBEDIENCE is what caused their heavenly clothes to evaporate and so reveal their nakedness. In the Qur'anic tradition, Adam and Eve were not naked, like in the Biblical story.

The story as told in Sura 7 is to make the clear point that whenever man disobeys God, he is exposed sooner or later. The nakedness of Adam and Eve became visible because they disobeyed the command of God, and not because of any inherent quality of the forbidden tree. At first God had made His own special arrangement to cover their nakedness, but when they disobeyed Him by eating the forbidden fruit, He undid that arrangement and they were left to cover themselves in their own way.

Finally, regarding human nature and the nature of revelations, yes, humans need both guidance and reform. Either one alone is insufficient. Revelations are God's covenants with various people via various messengers. Messengers come with a new book (covenant), whereas prophets only remind their people to uphold the book (covenant) already in their tradition. Jesus (pbuh) was a messenger; he came with a new scripture and a new law, and it was expected that the Children of Israel accept him and the law and obey God. However, he was the LAST messenger sent to the line of Israel. When most of the Hebrews rejected him, and even those who professed to follow his teachings went astray, God sent a messenger to the line of Ishamel (the Arabs).

This messenger was intended to be for all people, not just the Ishamelites. Muhammad ibn Abdullah of seventh century Arabia is considered this final messenger (pbuh).

Now as for the the nature of all these messengers, there ARE some differences in the specifics of the law from one community or Prophet to another. However, Islam teaches that the CORE of the message was always the same: "O People! God is ONE, and HE commands that you worship NONE but HIM."

The prophets not only received God's revelations, but they also molded their whole lives around those revelations. Prophets were role models whose words and deeds represent how to live a virtuous and God-conscious life. For this reason, the Qur'an teaches that whoever obeys the Prophet has obeyed God.

This was a really long email, even by my standards! Let me know your thoughts, and I look forward to continuing the conversation.

May peace be with you,
Ahmed

Email #16 – From: Chris
Sent: Sunday, March 6, 2016 5:39 p.m.

Greetings Ahmed!

I took another long time to respond. I've had a lot of my mind lately, and I apologize.

I find the jinn to be very interesting creatures. I wonder what their story is. Who was the first jinn to fall from grace? Was it Iblis? Are pious jinn present in the masjid on Fridays? It took an evil jinn to corrupt Adam, but what corrupts a jinn? It seems to be simply "pure bad energy." In my mind, I see something hard to write. But that thought makes me wonder if jinn cause man to fall, introducing their dark spiritual side into the pure spirit God gives us. But I don't think I could agree to that. It seems to hurt the idea of our free will.

Still, very interesting! Even Muslim scholars speculate on them, and talking to you, I have the impression that they don't usually like to leave things to speculation! I wonder if they angels were worried about them at their creation, just as they worried about Adam.

Regarding prophets and messengers, there is a smaller religion called the Baha'i faith. I'm certain you've heard about it. They claim that a man named Baha'u'llah is the second coming of Christ, much in the same metaphorical-but-not-really sense of John the Baptist being the second coming of Elijah.

I can't subscribe to it. However, it brings up the question of whether or not Muhammad is really the FINAL prophet. They also seems to relegate his status to prophet, as opposed to a "Manifestation of God," like Jesus and *Baha'u'llah*. They say that God sent many prophets to many people with many laws and books. They aren't the first to claim that, and indeed I find the addition of Krishna (!) into the list of prophets to be little hard to swallow. In fact, the last fellow with sizable following to claim that was Mani, founder of Manichaeism, which died out as a religion before the twentieth century.

But from a Muslim, how would you counter these claims?
-Chris

Email #17 – From: Ahmed Rashed
Sent: Friday, March 18, 2016 12:33 p.m.

In the Name of God; Most Gracious, Most Merciful:
Good afternoon, Chris:

The jinn are interesting. They are part of the unseen world, like angels, but have free will, like humans. It is how Islam explains all sorts of paranormal events (poltergeists, possessions, ghost sightings, haunting, psychic powers, black magic, etc.). We don't have any information about them before the creation of Adam. As for their influence on man, while it is true that the devils whisper temptations to people's hearts, our scholars remind us that the primary source of temptation is the person's own soul. In other words, human beings have both the capacity for good and evil, even if there were no jinn or Satan.

As for the Baha'i religion, it is not considered a branch of Islam. The litmus test for whether a person is considered Muslim or not is whether there is a belief or claim that directly contradicts a statement of Prophet Muhammad (pbuh). For example, the Prophet taught that angels exist and that Satan exists and that the Day of Judgment will happen. If somebody claimed that angels or Satan or Judgment Day were not really real (like the Prophet clearly said), then that person would be automatically excluded from the fold of Islam, even if they claim to believe in the Qur'an and the Prophet himself. The Prophet clearly stated that he was the final messenger and that God would not send any new prophets after him. Therefore, the Baha'i claim that Baha was the second coming of Jesus is rejected, and Baha'i are not considered Muslims.

The Prophet made clear prophecies about Jesus returning to Earth and establishing justice and God's Kingdom. However, unlike the Baha'i claims, Muhammad said Jesus would come down as JESUS, not someone else. He would have the same age as he did when God removed him from Earth to Heaven. He would have the same identity and information, and he would acknowledge Muhammad as the Last Prophet.

So while Muslims believe that Jesus will return to battle the False Messiah at the end of time, since the Baha'i statements do not match Prophet Muhammad's descriptions, they deny a critical part of Muhammad's message, and so we simply dismiss them.

May peace be with you,
Ahmed

Email #18 – From: Chris
Sent: Sunday, March 20, 2016 6:28 p.m.

Hello Ahmed!

Let me thank you again for this conversation. It's truly been beneficial for me, and I hope for you as well. These types of conversations require the utmost respect and I sincerely appreciate your comments.

I've tried having a similar one with the local imam where I live, but he hasn't been as responsive. I'm processing things and will have some thoughts to share back with you in the near future. Thank you again for all of your time and information thus far!
-Chris

Email #19 – From: Ahmed Rashed
Sent: Monday, March 21, 2016 9:45 a.m.

In the Name of God; Most Gracious, Most Merciful:
Good morning, Chris:
Glad to read that we are benefiting from this dialogue. Conversations like this are usually fraught with misunderstanding, so I am glad we can amicably discuss our beliefs in a nonconfrontational way. I look forward to your thoughts whenever you are ready.
May peace be with you,
Ahmed

With Dialogue Comes Understanding

A Message from the Author

"You will never understand a man until you walk a mile in his shoes."
I thank you for walking a mile with me on my journey of interfaith conversations. I would like to take this opportunity to share some reflections about these dialogues with you. This set of conversations is very precious to me because they show that there is hope for interfaith harmony and cooperation. I do not blame Muslims or Christians (or any group) for the situation we are in today. It is sad that we have to fight and kill each other in the name of religion, without ever trying to sit down and listen to one another like the followers of God we are supposed to be. I don't believe our Creator is pleased with such actions, and I admit to sometimes feeling very disappointed with my faith community for failing to live up to the teachings of our Prophet and the example of his Companions.

Many times we are blindsided by our negative emotions: fear, disappointment, anger, resentment, etc. We become intolerant of the shortcomings we see in others, but we don't look closely at ourselves. You will find that some of the best people you know are people of other faiths, and by "best people" I mean people who are ethical, caring, and altruistic; people who are civil and well-mannered. You will also find that some Muslims act just like the corrupt dictators that preside over their homelands. As Americans, we have been privileged to grow up in a First World country and raised on its high standards. No one chooses the family and country into which they were born. Most of the issues mentioned in this book stem from the dysfunction of the Third World countries in which Muslims were raised, not from the teachings of Islam itself.

The Prophet's (pbuh) trademark in dealing with people was mercy. At no point should Muslims have our noses in the air. We should focus on keeping a soft heart toward everyone, because this is what our Prophet taught. While it is true that many of today's Muslims are full of hate and rage, I would argue that MANY MORE, in fact the majority, are not this way.

They are quietly and humbly trying to live a God-conscious life and keep their families fed, educated, and well raised. That is why we always remind people that we must look to what Islam teaches at its source (Qur'an and Hadith) in order to judge, not what the followers of Islam do.

Humans make mistakes, often even critical and chronic ones, but the final arbiter is God ... not people. It is for this reason we see the wisdom of constant reminders and returning to the Book of God for spiritual renewal and rejuvenation. The rituals and worship of Islam are cyclical in that every day, week, month, and year there is a reminder to bring those who have become negligent or heedless of God can refresh their relationship with the Creator and become aware and grateful to God. On a daily basis, we have the ritual prayers and supplications. On a weekly basis, we have the Friday sermon and the recommended fasting. On a monthly basis, we have another set of recommended fasting and recommended night prayers. And on a yearly basis, we have the month of Ramadan and the month of Hajj. The Qur'an says, **"So remind, perhaps it will benefit the reminded."**

*****

If you enjoyed the book, please spread the word about it to your friends and contacts. If you have the time and inclination, it would be **great** if you would leave a review. Word of mouth is crucial for any author to succeed, so even if it is just a sentence or two, it would make all the difference and would be *very much* appreciated!

You can find more information and updates at our website WhatWouldAMuslimSay.net. Sign up to receive exclusive conversations that didn't make it into this book, free eBooks, my Islam101 slideshows, previews of upcoming books, and other relevant links and resources on Islam.

May peace be with you,
Ahmed Lotfy Rashed

Islamic Law, Theology, and Practice

What Would a Muslim Say?
Volume 4

by

Ahmed Lotfy Rashed

Coming September 2018

If you loved INTERFAITH DIALOGUES AND DEBATES *and can't wait for more, read on for a preview of the next book in the series.*

The next book contains three long, theological conversations with an atheist, a philosophy and religious studies professor, and a soul-searcher. This volume discusses Islamic history, Islamic law and practice, and Islamic theology and philosophy. It showcases many of the post-modern critiques of Islam and the responses to those critiques.

Here are the initial email questions to pique your interest!

Email #02 – From: Kayan
Sent: Monday, September 26, 2011 10:17 a.m.

I have a few questions around the verses in the Qur'an, and I hope you will be able to explain the rationale behind them.
1. Why is it claimed that Islam is the only true religion and that all other religions are false? If that is the case, how come Allah allows there to be more non-Muslims (Christians + Hindus + Buddhists + Atheists etc.) than Muslims in today's world?
2. **"There is no compulsion in religion."** This is an oft-quoted verse from the Qur'an to convince people of the tolerance in Islam to other religions. If this is true, why does Allah eternally torture and punish non-Muslims?
3. If Islam stands for peace and coexistence with other religions, how can one justify prophet Muhammad's destroying of idols in the Kaaba? How is that different from the recent Taliban bombing of the Bamiyan Buddha statues in Afghanistan?

Email #02 – From: David
Sent: Tuesday, July 21, 2015 1:30 p.m.

Hi Ahmed,

I teach religious studies, so I am familiar with Islam and especially its history. What I am curious about is *new thinking* in Islam. The biggest problem for any belief in Allah or God is the problem of evil. If we praise God for creation, then why do we not condemn God for causing so much suffering? If God is good, then why is there so much suffering? The modern world does not sustain the old defenses from the past; we know too much about how the world comes into being to believe old myths, and we know that we do not need a God for a moral universe. In fact, God only makes the universe less moral, because if we think of God as in control of creation, then God is the author of all this suffering. It makes no moral sense to worship a being that causes this amount of unjustified suffering.

Some will say the issue is the word "unjustified." How could we know what is justified from God's perspective? Fair enough, but that means that God is inexplicable and monstrous, because at any time incomprehensible suffering could be imposed on me with no reasonable explanation, from my point of view. On that account, God is random and malicious, not actually God. To claim that believing in God is good in this context is a moral absurdity; it is tantamount to worshiping chaos and misery.

Some will say the suffering is a consequence of decisions. But that does not explain the suffering caused by nature or in nature. It also fails utterly and completely once we notice that there is no good reason to believe that human beings actually make free decisions. Everything we know from science suggests free will is a useful illusion, hardly a defense of a God who causes suffering. What does Islam, what do modern Muslims say about these issues?

Thanks,
David

Email #02 – From: Rene
Sent: Saturday, March 4, 2017 4:24 a.m.

Hello Mr. Rashed:

Thank you for the information provided. I have several questions that I hope you will be able to answer.

1. In some places within the Qur'an, it is stated that righteous Jews, Christians, Sabeans, and Muslims will see Paradise. Yet another place contradicts this, stating that only those who believe in the final revelation, i.e., Islam, will be saved. Is there an official position on this?

2. How does Islam explain the crucifixion of Jesus? I have read several different answers to this question, which is why I pose it here. I have heard some say that it never happened to begin with; others say that someone resembling Jesus was crucified; some claim that he was crucified, did not die, but rather fainted; others still suggest that the crucifixion witnessed by the Jews who had him sentenced to death was a mass hallucination and did not really happen at all.
3. Some have told me that listening to music (other than *nasheeds*) is *haram*. Is this true? Obviously this would be the case for songs containing crude, profane, or suggestive or offensive lyrics, but what of those with completely innocent lyrics or songs that are instrumental only?
4. Do the references to jihad in the Qur'an only refer to spiritual warfare or literal but self-defensive warfare? There are passages alluding to ambushing polytheists (please correct me if I'm wrong), which is not indicative of self-defense.
5. What is the Islamic position on abortion? Or do views tend to differ in this area?
6. Does the Qur'an really condone a man striking his wife in Sura 4:34? I find it difficult to reconcile this concept with what I have been told a woman's position is within Islam. My understanding is that women, especially mothers, are elevated to a higher status. This does not seem to be in harmony with this particular verse.
7. I have read that the Qur'an permits men to sleep with female captives of war as well as slaves. I am beginning to read Qur'an in English, but I am by no means an expert, so please correct me if I am wrong on this.
8. I have heard Islam referred to as the "religion of peace" by Muslims. I understand that Islam's teachings, as well as much of the Qur'an, promotes peace, social justice, etc. — yet Islam was spread through wars, occupations, conquests of nations and kingdoms, etc. I don't understand how it can be claimed that it is peaceful when it was spread through such violent means.

9. I have read that apostasy in Islam is punishable by death in some Muslim-majority countries, despite the Qur'anic verse, **Let there be no compulsion in religion. Truth stands out clear from error.** Surely there are no verses or Hadiths condoning this?

    I was raised as a devout nondenominational Christian by a Church of Christ father and grandmother and a lapsed Roman Catholic mother. Religion has always played a very important role in my life, as has God and truth. Several years ago, I began studying my own religion as well as others closely — I am fascinated by religion, culture, and religious history. As someone who has studied the Bible as well as various Christian doctrines, I found inconsistencies in doctrine, tradition, and within the Bible itself. About a year ago, during a very dark time in my life (what is sometimes called a night of faith), when I was doubting Christianity more than ever but did not refute that there is a God, several of my friends who are Muslims began gently urging me to consider Islam. They taught me about the religion and suggested I read the Qur'an. Now, until they began to teach me about their beliefs, I knew only what has been propagated in the media: news stories and articles about the abhorrent actions of extremists. It was only when they shared their beliefs with me that I was able to see differently. After much studying, prayer, discussion, learning, etc., I am in a place where I will accept Islam if I can find answers to my questions, which I have related above.

    Thank you for any answers as well as for your time. I appreciate it very much.

    Sincerely,
    Rene

TOUGH QUESTIONS AND HONEST ANSWERS ABOUT THE WORLD'S FASTEST-GROWING AND MOST CONTROVERSIAL FAITH

TOP 15 TOUGH QUESTIONS ON ISLAM

AHMED LOTFY RASHED

Get your FREE copy when you sign up to the author's email list!

**GET IT HERE:
www.WhatWouldAMuslimSay.net**

MY TEACHER WAS AHMED RASHED. WE SPENT A LOT OF TIME GOING THROUGH THE QUR'AN. AFTER THAT I STARTED TO UNDERSTAND MUSLIMS MUCH BETTER.
—A FORMER ISLAM-101 STUDENT

About the Author

Ahmed Lotfy Rashed was born in Egypt and raised in Maryland. He studied physics at the University of Maryland Baltimore County. While there, he was on the Speakers Bureau for the Muslim Students' Association. He continued his education in Pennsylvania, earning his Masters' degree at Bryn Mawr College.

During his three years of graduate study, he served as Public Relations Officer for the Muslim Students' Association. It was at this time that Ahmed started talking about Islam at various churches, temples, and schools. He became known for his informal and approachable demeanor. His ability to break down complex religious and historical contexts for audiences earned him high reviews. He also taught math and science at the local Islamic School. In addition, he led the Youth Committee of the local mosque in Villanova. Soon after graduating, he married and found employment in Boston as a research engineer.

Since coming to Boston in 2004, he has been an active volunteer at several mosques in the Greater Boston Area. He has been the head instructor for the local Islam101 class since 2006. Also, he has been a volunteer for WhyIslam.org since 2009. He has presented Islam at schools and churches, and he has hosted visits to several major mosques in the area.

Ahmed continues to work and live in the Greater Boston Area with his wife and three children. In his spare time, he likes to read about comparative religions, Islamic law, Islamic history, and military history. He also has a weakness for fantasy and science fiction novels — a problem of which his wife is still trying very hard to cure him.

www.ingramcontent.com/pod-product-compliance
Lightning Source LLC
Chambersburg PA
CBHW070429010526
44118CB00014B/1960